ADVENTURES IN
DREAMING

Adventures in Dreaming: The Supernatural Nature of Dreams
by Justin Perry
Copyright ©2016
First Edition

Distributed by MorningStar Publications, Inc.,
a division of MorningStar Fellowship Church
375 Star Light Drive, Fort Mill, SC 29715

www.MorningStarMinistries.org
1-800-542-0278

ISBN— 978-1-60708-666-6; 1-60708-666-2

ADVENTURES IN
DREAMING

The Supernatural Nature
of Dreams

JUSTIN PERRY
Introduction by Rick Joyner

To LeeAnna:

Thanks for
dreaming with me.

CONTENTS

PREFACE

I n 2005, I felt an unusual unction to pray in the Spirit. For four hours at a time, I hid the clocks, unplugged the phone, and sipped water while pacing the floor and praying loudly. This was one of the greatest seasons of revelation in my life. I grew spiritually, began to see more healing and miracles, and dreamed more than ever before. During this season of powerful dreams and consistent revelation, I began to write *Adventures in Dreaming*.

As an avid reader, I am usually working through several books at a time. The shelves of my home and church office contain hundreds of books categorized according to topic. I do not have any books about dreams, however, nor have I read any. I have listened to a few teachings about dreams from well-known Christian leaders and studied dreams a bit in college psychology classes. For the past ten years, while working on this book, I felt a hesitation from the Lord any time I considered buying or reading a book about dreams. I believe it was important for me to finish this book before being significantly influenced by what others have written on this topic.

I do not assume that this book is completely unique or original, but there are concepts herein that I have never heard others speak of. This is not a book primarily about dream interpretation, although every chapter contains important interpretive keys. It is a book primarily about the supernatural nature of dreams. Dreams are a unique category of spiritual experience, manifold in their potential to change our lives and impact the natural and spiritual realms.

I have taught many classes and workshops on the content of this book. The most common feedback I have received is that people begin to dream more often and with greater intensity after receiving this teaching. I believe an impartation is available as you read and pray through the chapters. If you will knock, seek, and ask God for frequent, powerful, prophetic dreams, you will receive them.

Please take a moment to pray before proceeding:

Father, thank You for the gift of revelation. Please expand my capacity to receive this gift and faithfully steward it. Open the eyes of my spirit to see the invisible realm in my dreams. Let my heart be awake as I sleep, like the maiden in Song of Songs chapter five. As you did with King David, please instruct my heart in the night seasons. I desire to partner with You in prophetic ministry, spiritual warfare, and intercession even as I sleep. I now open my spirit to receive revelation and an impartation for life-changing dreams. Amen.

INTRODUCTION
BY RICK JOYNER

Justin has written an important book on what will soon be one of the important subjects of our times—dreams. Throughout the Scriptures we find dreams being used as a primary way for the Lord to speak to His people, and He has not changed. As we approach the end of this age Joel 2 and Acts 2 tell us that this will increase as the Holy Spirit is poured out. This is because in the "last days" we will need this kind of guidance.

Justin is well qualified to write this book. He has had considerable experience with dreams and with others who have been used this way. He is also an excellent teacher with a personal hunger for truth that compels him to search with depth and focus and then convey his findings with clarity applicable to our lives. Justin has also spent much of his Christian life in community with prophetic people given to dreams, visions, and prophecy. These have included some of the important prophetic voices of our times, such as Bob Jones, who was well known around the world for his prophetic gifts.

Justin has another crucial characteristic for being a teacher of such things—he is deeply devoted to the Scriptures and to sound doctrine. It seems that the level with which the Lord can trust us with prophetic revelation is linked to our depth of devotion to His written Word. Justin has a rare depth of love for the Scriptures, and he is contagious with it.

Dreams are one of the primary windows into the spiritual realm that God has given to us. Even so, just because something is spiritual does not mean it is from God. The dreams that do not come from the Holy Spirit can come from our own spirit, or at times, an evil spirit. Learning to discern between these is not difficult, but it is important. This book can help us easily discern these. As we build on these basics we can be used by God to communicate, and this is one of the most desperate needs in these times.

As the present communication by God to His people continues to grow in importance, we do need to deal with the fear factor that hinders so many of His people from hearing Him. Many Christians have more faith in the devil than in God. By this I mean that they have more faith in the devil to deceive them than they do in the Holy Spirit to lead them to the truth. The Lord Jesus promises that if we ask Him for a fish, He will not give us a serpent. If we ask Him for the real, we will not be given the counterfeit. That doesn't mean that the devil will not try to slip in some from him, but we will be far more prone to deception if we do not know the real. You cannot know what a counterfeit bill of currency looks like unless you know what the real looks like.

Because dreams are a window into the spiritual realm, they can also be used to release other forms of prophetic revelation in our life, such as visions, visitations, and other spiritual experiences. We call these "supernatural," but they should be natural for the new creation He has called us to be. As one of the ancients said, "We are not called to be natural beings that have occasional supernatural experiences, but rather supernatural beings that have occasional natural experiences." This is true. We are called to be more at home in the Spirit than we are in the natural.

This too is a process that comes with maturity. We grow with experience and in wisdom as we learn to interpret and apply our experiences correctly. I began having prophetic experiences immediately after I was born again, and I was even born again because of a supernatural experience. So, from the beginning of my Christian life, I was aware of the spiritual realm and the good and evil in it. However, I have found that this is the exception rather than the rule. I know many more who were gently introduced, mostly through dreams, and grow with experience. For many, just reading a book like this could open a whole new world in your relationship to the Lord and your impact in this life.

People commonly ask if they should ask the Lord for these experiences. I Corinthians 14:1 answers this: **"Pursue love, yet earnestly desire spiritual *gifts*, but especially that you may prophesy."** Many people claim to be open to having the Lord use them, but they never are. Why? If we don't value this enough to "earnestly" desire and pursue it, then we are not likely to be trusted with it. So how do we pursue the spiritual?

Reading a book like this is a good start. It's also a good way to grow in our spiritual gifts if we've already started. Those who rise to the top in just about any field are those whose passion for something keeps them in constant pursuit of it.

Another way to grow in spiritual gifts is to get around others with the same devotion. If you don't know any in your church or community, you may have to go to some effort to meet them. This effort will be worth it. Think about the effort it was for Barnabas to go and get Saul and then bring him back to Antioch with him. He did not have the Internet, or even a phone book, to find him. There are divine connections that we must make in order to be released into our own ultimate calling, just as they were. There are many prophetic conferences and a few places that have become prophetic gatherings. Making an effort to go to them and meet others is one way that we can earnestly seek the gifts.

Above all, keep in mind that **"the spirit of prophecy is the testimony of Jesus" (Revelation 19:10)**. Jesus is *"the* Prophet" that Moses spoke of and the One we are to grow up into. Our ultimate goal should never just be experiences, but experiences with Him so that we can behold His glory and be changed into His image. By this we can become better vessels through whom He can convey His messages. As Ephesians 1:10 tells us, **"all things will be summed up in Him."** So the ultimate goal of all we do should be to get closer to Him, to abide in Him, and to lead others to Him, not just to our gift. The Apostle Paul said it much better in one of the greatest prayers ever recorded:

For this reason I too, having heard of the
faith in the Lord Jesus which *exists* among
you and your love for all the saints,

do not cease giving thanks for you, while
making mention of *you* in my prayers;

that the God of our Lord Jesus Christ, the Father
of glory, may give to you a spirit of wisdom
and of revelation in the knowledge of Him.

I *pray* that the eyes of your heart may be
enlightened, so that you will know what is
the hope of His calling, what are the riches of
the glory of His inheritance in the saints,

and what is the surpassing greatness of His power
toward us who believe. *These are* in accordance
with the working of the strength of His might

which He brought about in Christ, when He
raised Him from the dead and seated Him
at His right hand in the heavenly *places,*

far above all rule and authority and power and
dominion, and every name that is named, not
only in this age but also in the one to come.

And He put all things in subjection
under His feet, and gave Him as head
over all things to the church,

which is His body, the fullness of Him
who fills all in all (Ephesians 1:15-23).

SECTION

I

WAKING UP TO THE
REALITY OF DREAMS

The dream life is as real as our waking
hours. Dreams were vital in biblical
times and they still are today.

1

THE SUPERNATURAL NATURE OF DREAMS

Often, our dreams are much more than a series of images and emotions passing through our minds—some are full-blown spiritual experiences. Scripture refers to dreams seven times as "night visions." They can be just as powerful and significant as an open vision. Dreams often have a greater purpose than merely communicating a message. Some are meant to change us, speak to us, or even accomplish something in the spiritual realm.

Has it ever occurred to you that when you dream of wrestling with or overcoming an enemy, you may actually be engaging in spiritual warfare? Have you ever considered that when you wake up from a dream and still feel the emotions and power of it, that something—good or bad—has influenced your soul? Have you ever wept deeply or prayed with your whole heart in a dream? Could it be that your spirit was actually engaging in intercession?

These questions query the supernatural nature of dreams. It is easy to miss the significance of a dream or other experience in the night if we are not paying attention to them. It is also possible to miss the significance of dreams if we merely try to interpret them. Some revelatory experiences we have during sleep are more than messages from God—some dreams are visitations of angels or of God Himself (see Matthew 1:20 and Genesis 20:3). Others impact the spirit of a person or even change their future (see Daniel 4:7 and Job 33:14–18).

HELP WITH UNDERSTANDING DREAMS

Dreams can be symbolic and often their true interpretation speaks something different than we initially understand. Sometimes an entire dream is from the Lord and other times only a portion of the dream is significant. Finally, some dreams require careful analysis to be understood, while others require only the overall message or gist to be comprehended.

Considering the above variables may cause one to ask, "How could I ever begin to understand my dreams when there are so many possibilities?" Fortunately, we have a Helper when interpreting dreams. His name is Holy Spirit. Remember that both Joseph and Daniel in the Bible repeatedly pointed to God as the source of their gift of interpretation (see Genesis 40:8 and Daniel 2:28). It was not just that these men were wise and full of understanding, they were friends of God with open ears, and God knows all things. We too can ask the Holy Spirit to give us understanding of our dreams. In the process, we will even get to know Him better. After all, we do not seek merely to know the meaning of dreams, but to know the One our dreams are meant to lead us to.

We are to seek the Lord to discover what our dreams mean. Apart from His guidance, dreams can be misleading or even harmful. As with every spiritual experience, we must have Jesus as our Guide and we must measure dreams against the Word of God. We recognize any dream or experience that leads us to act or think contradictory to Scripture as coming from another source. We will examine this kind of dream in a later chapter.

We must especially seek to understand dreams from God. These give us wisdom, guidance, warnings, and even revelation about what is to come. It is a grave mistake to ignore our dreams because they are among the clearest ways that God speaks to mankind. If we position ourselves to receive dreams and seek to understand them, they can help us stay on the path of life and reach our highest calling.

THE PROXIMITY PRINCIPLE

There is a concept we need to examine before continuing. When we "approach" something in the Spirit, we will often dream about it. This may be referred to as the "Proximity Principle." Let's observe a few examples of this principle in action.

When walking someone through a process of deliverance you may encounter the spirits that are harassing them in your dreams. This may be a result of spiritual attack—that the spirits are resisting you. Or it may simply be that your spirit begins to more accurately perceive the operation of these demons in your dreams. This is because you have come into close proximity of these spirits in your deliverance ministry.

On a more positive note, if you study angels in Scripture and seek to understand more about them, you will likely have more angelic activity in your dreams. Further, if you begin to spend time with prophetic people, or connect yourself to a ministry focused on the prophetic, you will likely experience an increase of dreams and visions. These manifestations are a result of spiritual proximity to angels or the prophetic anointing respectively.

The proximity principle also applies to geographic locations. For instance, if you are sleeping in a new city or in a new person's home, you may dream about the city or person. In such experiences, our spirit is more perceptive than our natural faculties. When we sleep, the distractions of our human nature are put aside and our spirit perceives the invisible realm. These dreams come as our spirit is in "proximity" to new places and people.

Several years ago, our home group spent six weeks studying the theology of "Revelatory Experience." I enjoyed those weeks of teaching and intentional focus on the "seer" experiences in Scripture. During this time, I began to see in the Spirit more clearly and to experience dreams and visions on a whole new level. In one week, I had three dreams where I saw an open vision within my dream. Each dream was important for me or for others close to me. I "approached" revelatory experience through study and meditation in Scripture, and revelatory experience began to manifest in my dreams.

As you study and meditate on the concepts in this book, it is reasonable to expect revelatory experiences to manifest in your life. This is not merely because you are thinking more about supernatural experiences and thus "psyche" yourself into having strange dreams. You will begin to experience more because you are seeking more. Jesus told us that if we seek, we will find; if we ask, we will receive; if we knock, the door will be opened to us (see Matthew 7:7). We are also told to "desire" or "covet" spiritual gifts (see I Corinthians 12:31 and 14:1, 39), especially prophecy. God tells us to pursue the prophetic gifts because He wants us to obtain them.

I want to encourage you to begin asking the Lord to activate your dream life and open the realm of revelatory experience to you. It is a good practice to ask Him every night to speak to you in dreams and give you understanding of them. Reading a book like this is a step in the right direction.

2

THE THEOLOGY OF DREAMS

Several years ago, I taught a group of young missionaries about the use of dream interpretation in evangelism. During a break, one of the leaders said to me, "I know there are a few references to dreams in the Bible, but is this really even worth talking about? It seems like such a small issue in the Word of God." His question was sincere, but thoroughly uninformed.

Scripture contains a vast amount of information about dreams and their interpretation. There are one hundred twenty-three references to dreams throughout the Bible (King James Version). At least twenty-one dreams are described in Scripture, most of which are interpreted. The Word of God is full of information about these spiritual experiences given during sleep.

Sixteen books of the Bible contain explicit information about dreams. That means one-fourth of God's Word pertains in some way to dreams. From the day of Abraham through the birth of the New Testament church and beyond, we see God consistently giving dreams to His people. This is not merely a fringe issue or hobby for prophetic people. Dreams are a significant, available, and beneficial means of revelation from God.

Each of the following biblical books contains references to or information about dreams:

- Genesis
- Numbers
- Deuteronomy
- Judges
- I Kings
- Job
- Psalms
- Song of Songs
- Ecclesiastes
- Isaiah
- Jeremiah
- Daniel
- Joel
- Zechariah
- Matthew
- Acts

From the passages in these books, some of which we will examine later, it is clear that God has always spoken to His people through dreams and always will. He gave dreams as a way of speaking to His friends and His enemies, to guide them, change them, and even show them things that would happen in the future.

Fundamental Christianity prescribes that we believe the Bible is true and that God spoke through dreams in ancient times. However, the questions some would debate are: Does He speak through dreams today? Will He speak to me in dreams?

DREAMS ARE FOR TODAY

The Scriptures teach us that there will be an outpouring of the Holy Spirit accompanied by dreams and visions in the last days before Jesus returns. Peter spoke of this in Acts 2:

> **And it shall come to pass in the last days, says God, that I will pour out of My Spirit on all flesh; your sons and your daughters shall prophesy, your young men shall dream dreams. And on My menservants and on My maidservants I will pour out My Spirit in those days; and they shall prophesy (Acts 2:17).**

This passage is clear that in the last days, God will pour out His Spirit with manifestations of dreams and visions. The closer we get to the end of this age, the more dreams God will give to mankind. He loves to reveal Himself, and these revelatory experiences are a major way in which He does this.

All over the earth there is a surge of interest in dreams and visions. Many people, Christians and unbelievers, are having these supernatural experiences. As we will examine later, countless people are now coming to Christ because God has revealed Himself in dreams.

If God is pouring out His Spirit on all flesh and giving dreams and visions to young and old people everywhere, how much more should the sons and daughters of

God expect to receive them? In these days, God will reveal Himself and His purposes to His people.

DREAMS: DIVINE INTERVENTION

In the thirty-third chapter of Job we find this revelation about dreams:

> **For God may speak in one way, or in**
> **another, yet man does not perceive it.**
>
> **In a dream, in a vision of the night, when deep**
> **sleep falls upon men, while slumbering**
> **on their beds,**
>
> **then He opens the ears of men,**
> **and seals their instruction.**
>
> **In order to turn man from his deed,**
> **and conceal pride from man,**
>
> **He keeps back his soul from the Pit, and his life**
> **from perishing by the sword (Job 33:14-18).**

This passage tells us the Lord is actively engaged in speaking to humanity. He will speak **"one way, or in another, yet man does not perceive it."** He will attempt to get through to the heart of a person, even if they are not paying attention to His voice. Often, in these situations, God gives **"a dream . . . a vision of the night"** during sleep. In these dreams, He opens the ears of men and gives them instruction.

Specifically, God **"seals their instruction."** The idea is that He does not necessarily give information that is easy to understand at first. He will often give information that seems to be "sealed" or covered over. The dream is like a message in an envelope that must be opened before one can understand the contents. This requires us to draw near to Him and ask for understanding. This humbles us, or "conceals pride," causing us to depend on Him.

There are other ways in which dreams sometimes seem "sealed." Have you ever had a dream that you knew was important, but you could not remember, or you only remembered a small portion? Sometimes as the day continues and you pray about it, or maybe as you tell someone else about it, it seems to slowly come back to your mind. It is almost as though the dream is slowly being "unsealed" as you remember it.

Doug Addison, a prophetic teacher, says that the phenomenon known as "déjà vu" could also stem from "sealed" dreams. When we have this strange feeling, it may be that we *have* experienced this moment or situation before. Perhaps we saw the circumstance in a dream. In light of this, I have learned to ask the Lord what I should do each time I have the feeling of "déjà vu." This practice has positioned me to receive wisdom from the Lord during some of life's key moments.

Finally, this passage in Job says that in dreams, God **"keeps back his soul from the Pit, and his life from perishing by the sword."** This means that there are times when God gives people dreams to save their lives. This was the case with Abimelech after he took Sarah into his house in Genesis 20. The Lord warned him that if he did not give Sarah back to Abraham, he was a dead man. This is also what happened in Acts 27 when an angel came to Paul at night (possibly in a dream). The angel gave Paul instructions on how to save the lives of everyone on the ship.

God is ultimately kind and merciful, and He will go to any length to reach us and speak to us. He is a redeemer by nature. Dreams are one of the glorious means of His redemption.

3

THE DREAM LIFE

I once read a story[1] about a boy who lived two lives. He lived one life while he was awake and another in his dreams. While awake, he was just another boy, but in his dreams, he was great and powerful. It turns out that his dreams were actually ancestral memories—he was dreaming of things that happened thousands of years ago.

The possibility of supernatural experiences in dreams is compelling. Could it be possible for us to see the past or the future in dreams? Furthermore, could it be possible to have a "dream-life" that is consistently significant for our waking lives? We will consider these and other questions in this chapter.

YOUR DREAM LIFE

---

1   *Before Adam* by Jack London. This book is interesting, but unfortunately it promotes the theory of evolution.

The idea that we can dream about things that have happened in history makes logical sense. As descendants of Adam, each of us has a lineage traceable to the origins of mankind. Thus, we somehow carry the events of human history in our DNA. It is reasonable that I could dream of a great battle in the Revolutionary War if an ancestor of mine fought in it.

In the same way, it makes sense that a born-again believer can dream accurately about the future. If God knows the end from the beginning (see Isaiah 46:10), then He knows everything that will happen in the future. If this All-knowing and Eternal God lives in us, then we can dream about things that have not yet happened on earth. God gives dreams that foretell the future. He also gives dreams to warn of things that could happen if we do not respond appropriately.

Our dream life is crucially important. It is possible to have such an active dream life that it becomes a major component of our existence. Our sleep can become a time of supernatural experience on a regular basis—like another life we live out while we lie in bed. Our dream life can become a major source of inspiration, direction, healing, and empowerment.

King David spoke of his dream-life in this way:

I will bless the LORD who has given
me counsel; my heart also instructs me
in the night seasons (Psalm 16:7).

You have tested my heart; You have visited

**me in the night; You have tried me and
have found nothing (see Psalm 17:3).**

David encountered God in the night, most likely through dreams. These dreams brought him counsel and changed his heart.

The Shulamite in Song of Solomon 5:2 says of her dream life, **"I sleep, but my heart is awake."** Her heart was "awake," or spiritually aware, even while she slept. She experienced revelation in the middle of the night.

Our prayer to God should be that our own dream lives are activated in this way. As Rick Joyner has often prayed at prophetic conferences, "Lord, we don't want to waste a single moment—not even in our sleep!"

MY DREAM LIFE

Practically every significant change or development in my life as a believer has been foretold in dreams. The Lord has given my family and me dreams of major events, such as moving to different states or changing professions. We have also received dreams about less consequential matters, such as how to interact with specific people in relationships. I have an active dream life, and it has become one of the primary ways I receive direction from God.

I once dreamed of being back in college and enrolled in three classes. Each class was a subject I previously felt the Lord leading me to pursue for personal growth. Shortly afterwards, I had the same dream, only this time I was behind in all three courses and had missed class often.

When I awoke, I knew each subject was important to my life and development, but I was not making the time to pursue them. After some serious prayer and discussion with my wife, we came to an agreement. For a season, I would cut back my hours at work and spend fifteen hours a week studying these three topics. I would treat them exactly as if I were enrolled full-time in college again.

Periodically, for the next several months, I dreamed of being in class again. I would receive progress reports from my teacher, giving me grades in each subject. A couple of times my attendance grade in one of the subjects was low. This coincided with the way I had neglected that particular topic in the previous weeks.

This may seem unbelievable to some or trivial to others, but to me it was a beautiful season of interaction with God in my dream life. I was blessed to have clear communication from heaven about specific things God was calling me to do. During this period of about six months, I learned a great deal about time management and about being a disciple. I learned firsthand what it meant to be enrolled in the school of the Holy Spirit.

Dreams often serve as a kind of "progress report." Whether dreams are from the Lord, the soul, or even the enemy, they can be an accurate indicator of our spiritual progress. If we have cluttered our soul with too many distractions and images, our dreams may become cluttered and incoherent. If there is a door opened, where the enemy has access, we may experience fear, lust, or darkness in our dreams. Finally, if we are drawing nearer to the Lord, we may see and experience heaven in our dreams.

MARRIED DREAM LIFE

My wife LeeAnna's dream life and my own are insep-
arably connected. This is understandable considering that
we are "one flesh" and are "cleaving" to one another (see
Genesis 2:24). Several times we have had similar dreams
in the same night. We have also each received part of the
answer to a question we had asked the Lord. When we put
our dreams together, we had a complete answer.

There was a period of several months when LeeAnna
was having detailed dreams about me every week, only
she did not know it. She would wake up and say, "I just
had the strangest dream" and would describe detailed
symbolic dreams that meant nothing to her. I would sit
and try to maintain composure as the Lord gave me clear
interpretation of these dreams, which were mostly correc-
tion for me.

This particular season was a difficult time in my life.
It is possible that in the midst of my struggle, I was not
giving a place for the Lord to speak to me (see Job 33:14-
18). In His mercy, He spoke to me through my wife in
such a way that only I understood. The corrective words
cut like a surgeon's knife at the issues in my heart. Since
LeeAnna did not realize the dreams were for me, she had
no problem sharing them, holding nothing back. I had
no problem receiving them because I knew they were the
Lord's words, not my wife's.

I use these personal stories not to call attention to my
own dream life but as illustrations. Nearly every night for
twelve years, LeeAnna and I have asked the Lord to speak

to us in dreams. God is faithful to answer this prayer. Unity in marriage is powerful and so is married dream life.

Our dream lives can bring tremendous blessing, heavenly guidance, and an indication of our spiritual progress. May the Lord activate our dream lives as never before.

SECTION

II

UNDERSTANDING THE NATURE OF DREAMS

Dreams are a powerful category of spiritual experience. They reveal the invisible realm, foretell the future, fight spiritual battles—even transform lives.

4

MESSAGES FROM HEAVEN

Diverse supernatural experiences await the "awakened" dreamer. You can be positioned to receive revelation and interact with angels when your dreams are sanctified by the Holy Spirit. Like that of Daniel, or Joseph the father of Jesus, an activated dream life manifests God's strategy into the earth.

Now that we have laid a foundation for understanding the nature of dreams, it is important to understand that dreams are often prophetic, revelatory, and strategic. Perhaps more importantly, dreams are in a category of spiritual experience all their own. Many encounters in the night are not merely communicating information—they accomplish something in the invisible realm. Powerful intercession, timely healing, and victorious spiritual warfare have been accomplished while God's people sleep.

To help clarify the manifold experiences given in the night, we will now examine various categories of dreams. I have cataloged them using descriptive language in the proceeding chapters. While I expect some overlap to occur and my words to fall short of properly describing these ethereal realities, understanding these distinctions will better equip us to enjoy a fruitful dream-life.

Let's take a look at the first category, dreams that contain a message.

MESSAGE DREAMS

"Message dreams" are dreams that contain a message or a word from God to you, like a message in a bottle from heaven. These are among the most common type of prophetic experience. One of God's names is The Word, and He is constantly communicating to us. Many of the dreams recorded in the Bible were given to convey a message to the dreamer. As with the ancients, many saints today receive the word of the Lord as they sleep. Consider Psalm 16:7: **"I will bless Jehovah, who hath given me counsel; Yea, my heart instructeth me in the night seasons" (ASV).** Message dreams give counsel and instruction from the Lord.

Often the message contained is for you; other times the message is for someone else. As a general principle, the Lord will give you dreams for people with whom you have access to share them. For example, if you were to dream about the President of the United States and you have no access to communicate with him, the dream is likely for the purpose of intercession. Maybe the President is symbolic, and the dream contains a message for you.

Message dreams are a broad category of dream. There is some overlap with prophetic, warning, and visitation dreams as those often contain a message. Message dreams are often symbolic and require interpretation to be fully understood. In a future chapter, I will give some detail about interpreting symbols in dreams, although that is not the main purpose of this book. For now, it is sufficient to know the Lord speaks to each of us in a language we can understand.

God sometimes conveys His messages using symbols and parables that mean something to us, even if they do not mean anything to anyone else. We call these "personal symbols." He also uses "contemporary symbols," those that are universally understood in a particular culture. For instance, a dog could be symbolic of companionship, and an army tank could allude to warfare. Finally, the Lord uses symbols from the Bible, the purest communication from God to man. Many symbols, numbers, and colors show up in Scripture repeatedly, and the contexts of these appearances give explanation to the symbol. We refer to these as "biblical symbols."

Message dreams may require interpretation more often than other categories of dreams. We interpret to extract the message so that we can receive it ourselves or communicate it to someone else. There is good news, however, about interpretation—the One who gives the dream will help us to understand it.

GROWING IN INTERPRETATION

If we desire to grow in dream interpretation, we must grow in the knowledge of the Lord and His Word. The better acquainted we become with Him, the more accustomed we become to His language. The Lord tells us, **"For My thoughts *are* not your thoughts, nor *are* your ways**

My ways, says the Lord" (Isaiah 55:8). Conventional wisdom and human understanding will get us nowhere in our pursuit of the knowledge of God. We need to grow in the Spirit of revelation to grow in interpretation.

Knowing the voice of God is far better than knowing all the symbols in a dream dictionary. Our greatest resource in interpreting dreams is asking Him what they mean. God delights to speak to us, and He delights in our speaking to Him. Our dreams can be His means of drawing us to speak to Him.

A new believer who has never studied symbolism or dream interpretation can be an effective dream interpreter. A relationship with the Holy Spirit and a basic understanding of the nature of dreams is all that is needed to understand their meanings. As we become more familiar with the voice of God, we begin to hear Him whispering the interpretation into our ear while someone shares his or her dream with us.

As we seek to interpret our own dreams, consider sharing them with other spiritually-minded Christians, especially those gifted in interpretation (see Daniel 1:17). It is astonishing how we begin to understand our dreams in the process of describing them to someone else. Others often see things about our dreams that we miss, due to our biases or "blind spots."

WHO IS YOUR DREAM FOR?

One of the first steps in understanding a message dream is discerning whom it is for. Often when we have a dream where someone else is the main focus, there is a message for him or her in the dream. We must ask the Lord for wisdom in handling a dream about someone else. At times, we should share the whole dream with them, while at other times we may share only the interpretation. There are certainly times when it would be best to keep the dream to ourselves and intercede for the person. Think of Joseph's first two dreams in Genesis 37. These dreams were not only about him, but also about his family. Joseph's dreams were certainly accurate, but it is questionable whether he should have shared them with his family. God may have intended to speak to Joseph about his future without revealing it to his brothers and parents.

Dreams can have a multi-dimensional application. If I have a dream that seems to be primarily for someone else, it does not mean there is nothing in it for me. In Daniel 7, Daniel receives an epic dream of world events that would unfold long after his own lifetime. The dream was primarily for his nation and proceeding generations of God's people. Most of the dream was about kings and kingdoms with which he would have no personal interaction. However, we can assume this dream gave Daniel great personal confidence. It must have strengthened him to boldly stand as an intercessor for his nation and a prophet to godless authorities. He saw in this dream that although beast-kings would prevail for a time, ultimately God would overthrow them all. In the end, God would triumph over the powers of evil and give the kingdoms of earth to His people. Daniel lived in light of this revelation the rest of his days.

5

ASKING INTERPRETIVE QUESTIONS

We will now consider some interpretive questions that serve as a good starting point for interpreting dreams. These questions are helpful in seeking to understand any sort of visionary-prophetic experience, but they are especially useful in understanding message dreams. Here are six questions to ask a dreamer when interpreting their experience:

1. WHO WAS IN THE DREAM?

Could any of the people in your dream signify an idea God is speaking to you about? For instance, in dreams a person's earthly father can symbolize God, their heavenly Father. Or in a more general sense, if someone dreams of Bob Jones, a great prophet of this generation, the dream may be about the prophetic ministry rather than about Bob.

At times, a person's name is the key to understanding a dream. I recently dreamed of a man, Joshua Freeman, whom I have not seen for over ten years. The Lord used his name to speak to me about Joshua possessing the Promised Land, a theme our leadership team has been hearing for some time. His last name, Freeman, was also an important part of the revelation. God began to speak to me about true grace, the grace of the New Covenant. True grace does not set us free to sin; it sets us free *from* sin. Only when someone walks in this biblical grace does he become a "free man."

It is helpful to ask, "What is the first thing that comes to mind when I think of the person in that dream?" Perhaps they are incredibly talented musically, or they are a powerful intercessor. The dream may be a message to you about music or intercession, rather than about that person. It could also be that someone in your dream is obnoxious or offensive to you. In such cases, the Lord may be using this person to highlight something in you that He desires to change. It is easier to see a flaw in someone else, even if we are blind to the issue in our own life (see Matthew 7:1–5).

2. WHERE DID THE DREAM TAKE PLACE?

The dream's setting is often the key to interpretation. If you dream of playing chess with a friend on the deck of a cruise ship, you would approach the dream differently than if you were playing chess in a dungeon. If your dream takes place in a hospital, the theme may have to do with healing or restoration. If it takes place on the mall in Washington, D.C., the dream probably has to do with government. If we can identify what the setting or location may signify, it will greatly aid in interpreting the dream.

3. WHERE WERE YOU SLEEPING AND WHO WAS WITH YOU WHEN YOU HAD THE DREAM?

In an earlier chapter, I wrote of the Proximity Principle. This phenomenon occurs when you dream of something or someone you are in close proximity to. It is important to pay attention to your dreams when you are in a new place for the first time. God commonly gives prophetic people dreams about the city or even the home in which they are sleeping.

Your spirit is sensitive to the invisible realm around you. When you sleep, many of the distractions of your waking life are put aside and your spirit is permitted to accurately perceive the spiritual atmosphere. When staying in someone else's home, your dreams may reflect what is going on in the lives of your hosts. Similarly, when you sleep in a new city or nation for the first time, you may have a prophetic dream about that location. Simply being aware of this possibility may help you to understand strange dreams you may have while traveling.

4. HOW DID YOU FEEL IN THE DREAM?

In our waking lives, our emotions may give an accurate indication of reality. Other times, they can be very misleading. If we allow our emotions to guide us each day, we may often end up at the wrong destination. However, emotions can be an accurate compass in dream interpretation. Reflecting on how we felt in a dream can help us discern its source and also the direction to follow in interpretation.

If you were flooded with hope when you stepped into a building in a dream, the interpretation will likely be positive. If you felt as though you were in danger when you walked into the building, the dream may be a warning from God. People often feel the presence of God in a prophetic dream. Sometimes these dreams are the result of angelic visitation or an encounter with God during sleep.

Identifying how we felt in a dream can give us a nudge in the right interpretive direction. Due to the subjective nature of emotions, I would like to reiterate that God is our greatest resource in seeking to understand a dream (see Genesis 40:8). He loves to speak to us, and He uses dreams to draw us into closer communication with Him.

5. HAVE YOU BEEN ASKING GOD TO SPEAK TO YOU ABOUT ANYTHING SPECIFIC?

If you have been asking God a question, expect the answer to come in a dream. If the imagery of a dream is symbolic and seemingly unrelated to the question you asked, it is possible to miss your answer. Sometimes at a glance, a dream appears to have little to do with its interpretation. How easy would it have been for Joseph to miss the interpretation of the baker's dream in Genesis 40? How would Daniel have interpreted Nebuchadnezzar's dream in Daniel 4 without the help of a revelatory angel?

We must consider our dreams as valuable as treasure. If someone gave us a map to uncover a buried fortune, we would pursue the destination on the map until we were satisfied. In the same way, when we receive a dream that seems unrelated to anything "on our radar," we should pursue the Lord until we are satisfied that we understand it or that it was not from Him (see Proverbs 25:2).

6. ARE THERE ANY UPCOMING EVENTS OR MINISTRY TRIPS THAT GOD MAY BE SPEAKING TO ME ABOUT?

God is remarkably faithful to equip us for the things He has called us to do. He often speaks to us about things in the future that we have not asked Him about. God will especially speak to us about upcoming ministry opportunities to ensure we have something to give. He is eager to minister to His people. If you are planning a trip, party, or even dinner with a neighbor, you may receive strategic insights from God. In Isaiah 42:9, God declares, **"Behold, the former things are come to pass, and new things do I declare; before they spring forth I tell you of them"** (**ASV**).

LeeAnna and I once spent the weekend with a couple we have known since college. We love them dearly, but they are rather opposed to Christianity. The night before they arrived in town, I had a dream about the wife that was related to her gifts and calling. I shared the dream at breakfast the first morning we were together. She was significantly impacted by the dream, and we spent the first few hours of the day talking about pursuing our personal calling from God. When our friends traveled home to Georgia the next day, they talked for hours about pursuing their passions and callings. They made a decision to quit their high paying jobs in Atlanta and devote their lives to discovering their purpose.

Less than two years later, the husband enrolled in Berklee College of Music in Boston and the wife stepped into an entirely new career field. They jokingly remind me each time we talk, "Justin, it's all your fault." They have received dreams from the Lord as well. We have since been able to share with them that true fulfillment comes from being in the will of God, rather than being in the right career.

All this came about because God gave me a dream the day before our friends came to visit. I had not even thought to ask for a word for them, but the Lord wanted to impact this couple. They have not yet accepted Jesus, but He is pursuing them!

6

DREAMS THAT SEE INTO THE SOUL OR SPIRIT

When we sleep, it is as if the natural part of our mind is put aside. This is why the Lord can speak in a dream, even when our lives and minds are too cluttered for us to hear Him through other means. Romans 8:7 tells us, **"The carnal mind is enmity against God . . . it is not subject to the law of God."** This means that a mind not submitted to the Holy Spirit will actually resist God and His revelation. It seems that many spiritual dreams are received merely because the carnal mind is asleep or inactive. This allows our spirit to be more perceptive, without the distractions of waking life. Thus, in dreams we hear from God and see into the spiritual realm.

Having just considered "message dreams" and questions for interpreting them, we will now explore another category—dreams that see into the spiritual realm.

SLEEPING WITH AN AWAKENED HEART

Previously, we considered Song of Solomon 5:2, where the Shulamite describes her experience in the night:

"I sleep, but my heart is awake." When we sleep, our heart, or our spirit, remains awake. At times, it is as though our spirit man sits up and takes a look around while we sleep. We then behold the invisible realm in our dreams.

As previously discussed, sometimes when sleeping in a new place, your dream will reveal what is taking place in the spirit in that location. You may see things that are happening in the lives of the people who live there. You may also have a symbolic dream of the spiritual situation in the city or nation. In the same way, when you stay the night in someone's home, you may dream about him or her, or even the history of the home or geographic location.

In 2004, when my wife and I moved into a new apartment, we both felt the spiritual atmosphere was "heavy" or "cloudy." I had three dreams in our first five nights that contained the same theme. The dreams seemed to reveal that a previous resident of the apartment had been neglected and emotionally abused. While sharing the dreams with my sister, she reminded me that the apartment was built to accommodate someone in a wheelchair. I felt my dreams were about a disabled person who previously lived in the apartment. For the next several days, I was burdened for this person and prayed for them often. I asked the Lord to heal their heart and lead them to salvation. LeeAnna and I also anointed the entire apartment with oil, consecrating it to God and asking Him to fill every room. After a few days of this intercession, the heaviness lifted and the dreams stopped.

In this example, my spirit man identified demonic spirits of neglect and rejection lingering in our new home. I perceived the revelation from my spirit as a dream and was, therefore, equipped to pray with understanding. These sorts of dreams are not necessarily revelation directly from God as much as they are an operation of the gift of discerning of spirits (see I Corinthians 12:10). These dreams can be very useful for intercession.

THE INVISIBLE UNVEILED

In 2010, immediately after I assumed leadership of MorningStar's Healing Teams, I experienced some remarkable things. Several times in the first week of leading our teams, I saw (with my eyes open) a healing angel standing next to me. He was seven feet tall, silver, and full of electricity. I was also awakened in the morning several times by the sound of a golden bell ringing. In Scripture, the high priest wore golden bells on the hem of his garment so Israel could hear him moving in the Most Holy Place. I knew this was a sign that "the High Priest was on the move," and He was answering our prayers for healing.

During this same week, I also had two remarkable experiences in the night. The first night, I saw the faces and heard the voices of countless people crying out for healing. There were people with cancer asking God to touch them, mothers praying for their children, and people who did not even know God asking Him for help. The power of God was being released for healing in response to these prayers.

The second night, I saw the faces and heard the voices of countless people cursing the body of Christ. Some were involved in the occult and were sending sickness to Christians. Others were Christians who were cursing their fellow believers without realizing it. They were criticizing and gossiping and praying soulish prayers. These curses released demonic sickness in the same way the godly prayer mentioned above released healing.

I experienced these things because I was given a new place of authority and access to new realms in the Spirit. I was experiencing some significant things while awake, but in my dreams I saw both sides of the spiritual battle in which I was enlisted. Since I was given this new place of responsibility, my spirit was positioned to perceive the momentum of prayer for healing and the enemy's resistance to healing.

Our dreams are an unparalleled resource in discerning the invisible realm. Let us pursue God for greater revelation in our dreams and for the grace to be faithful to rightly respond to what we see.

7

PROPHETIC DREAMS

O
ur dreams may foretell the future. In the New Testament, the Greek word *prophētēs* and its cognates have to do with forth-telling, or telling the future. Prophetic dreams reveal what is to come. This category of dreams is a powerful gift from God.

Think of the prophetic dreams surrounding the birth of Jesus. When Joseph was ready to break the engagement with Mary, he was told about the future. He was told that his fiancé's pregnancy was **"of the Holy Spirit . . . and she will bring forth a Son, and you shall call His name JESUS, for He will save His people from their sins" (see Matthew 1:20–21).** The Magi were warned in a dream that if they traveled east by the same road they came, there would be trouble from Herod (see Matthew 2:12). Joseph was prompted in a dream, **"Arise, take the young Child and His mother, flee to Egypt . . . for Herod will seek the young Child to destroy Him" (see Matthew 2:13).** He was later told in a dream to return to

Israel (see Matthew 2:20). The Father released prophetic dreams to prepare the way for His Son.

INTO THE FUTURE

The Book of Daniel gives us clear examples of prophetic dreams. King Nebuchadnezzar and Daniel both had dreams that spoke of the future (see Daniel 2 and 7). One of Nebuchadnezzar's dreams foretold his own seven-year fall into insanity (see Daniel 4). These two men saw events that would come to pass beyond their own day, some of which would unfold in the last generation.

Daniel explained a major purpose of prophetic dreams to the king: **"There is a God in heaven who reveals secrets, and He has made known to King Nebuchadnezzar what will be in the latter days" (see Daniel 2:28).** God is a "revealer of secrets" and He desires to make the future known. Specifically, He wants His people to be ready for the "latter days," a biblical moniker for the final days preceding the second coming of Christ. These dreams of the "latter days" could be called "eschatological dreams" or dreams pertaining to the events in biblical eschatology (the study of the end times).

MY FIRST PROPHETIC DREAM

One night, a month or so after I accepted Jesus as Lord, I was sitting on my bed reading in the Bible of Joseph's experiences with dreams and interpretation. Completely unfamiliar with prophetic dreams, I asked God a question before I went to sleep. "Why don't You speak to people in dreams anymore?" I then turned out the light and fell asleep.

That night I dreamed I was walking in the mall with a friend. A tall, thin young man walked by us and said something offensive to my friend. I snapped back, "Hey man, watch your mouth!" The character in my dream spun around and looked at us with crazy eyes and said, "Listen, you don't know what I'm going through! I'm so strung out on drugs that I can't eat or sleep. It's destroyed my family, and I've lost my wife. My life is ruined!" My heart filled with compassion. I told him that God had delivered me from addiction and the Lord would deliver him too if he was willing. I asked him for his phone number and as he wrote it down, his hands shook intensely. I also handed him my phone number and said, "If you're serious about getting your life turned around, give me a call."

I then woke up to the phone ringing. Half asleep, I answered the phone. A friend on the other line (we'll call him Mike) said, "Hey man, come over to the hotel. I've got some drugs and a cooler full of beer."

Mike was at a hotel because his wife kicked him out of the house after finding his stash of drugs, again. He was literally at the end of his rope and had lost his family and wife, just like the guy in my dream. Although he called to invite me to party with him, he really only wanted someone to keep him company and minister to his broken heart. As you will recall, the last words I spoke in my dream were, "If you are serious about getting your life turned around, give me a call." When I woke up, the phone was ringing, and it was my friend calling for help.

I got to share with Mike that I did not drink or do drugs anymore because God had given me something much better in my relationship with Jesus. I shared the Gospel with him and took a Bible to his hotel, which he later called to tell me that he had been reading. Nearly seven years later, he accepted Jesus as Savior. God gave me a prophetic dream to prepare me for Mike's call, and I was able to have a tremendous impact on his life.

Did God know my friend would need to hear the Gospel that desperate morning? Of course He did. He looked through time and saw an opportunity to share the words of life with Mike, and He looked for someone who would speak them. God led me to read about Joseph's dreams and ask Him about them to set the stage for my dream and the proceeding phone call.

Since that morning, I have sought to understand my dreams and to realize when the Lord is speaking to me. Nearly every night before we go to sleep, my wife and I ask the Lord to speak to us in dreams and give us understanding of them. Much of our life together has been prophesied ahead of time in these dreams.

DREAMS OF DESTINY

There is a sub-category of prophetic dreams, which I will call "Dreams of Destiny." These dreams help to equip you for your ultimate destiny. You may have dreamed of tremendous scenes involving feats of faith or ministry. These are dreams of preaching to millions of people, raising the dead, walking on water, flying, even fighting impossible battles and winning. These dreams have a feeling of engaging in something far bigger than ourselves, defying the limitations we normally experience.

Many have dreamed of catastrophic events unfolding in the earth. These dreams reveal devastated cities, nuclear war, global anarchy, and chaos. Often in the midst of these scenes, the dreamer plays an important role—maybe helping others, moving in supernatural ministry, or perhaps just witnessing the chaos. Either way, dreams of destiny are mostly preparation for our soul and spirit and for what will eventually unfold in the earth. Some of these dreams may resemble the eschatological dreams mentioned above. Extreme dreams involve intense imagery and produce extreme emotions. Processing such imagery and emotion is important in training us for our future.

To illustrate the need for such preparation, allow me to reference the content of chaplaincy training. One of the primary focuses of chaplaincy courses is to teach future chaplains how to function in the midst of crises. The courses emphasize the importance of being emotionally prepared in the midst of catastrophic situations. Although some things can only be learned by experiencing a crisis, it can be a great help to role-play and talk through traumatic scenarios in the classroom.

In the same way, dreams of destiny can be helpful in preparing us for intense situations we have not yet experienced. If you have vividly dreamed of an extreme scenario, you have already encountered some of the intense imagery and feelings of such an environment.

FAITH FOR THE FUTURE

Another way dreams of destiny prepare us is by imparting faith. When we see ourselves thriving and moving in power in impossible situations, we receive a measure of faith for these situations.

Consider Hebrews 11:1, **"Now faith is the substance of things hoped for, the evidence of things not seen."** If we have seen something prophetically or "by faith," it is as though we have "evidence" that it exists—it has "substance" before it manifests in the natural realm. If I dream of raising the dead and multiplying food in the midst of a devastated city, I have evidence (and a measure of faith) that I can do this. If I have experienced being the CEO of a multi-billion dollar business in my dream, then I have access to faith for something equally as tremendous to happen in my future. Though we may never walk out the exact scenarios in our dreams, these dreams of destiny prepare us for the "impossible" exploits God has planned for our future. They impart faith and help to transform us into people who are ready for immense possibilities.

SUSTAINING FAITH

Consider Joseph's dreams of destiny. He saw the sun, moon, and stars bowing down to him. He saw himself in a position of such great authority and influence that even his older brothers would someday bow down to him. Joseph's dreams began God's process of changing him into the man who could be entrusted with a remarkable destiny. Eventually, Joseph's dream came true, and he became the second most powerful man in the world. Everyone, including his older brothers, bowed down to him.

Genesis 37–47 tells us that Joseph had a difficult journey to the fulfillment of his dream. He was tossed into a pit, pawned as a slave, promoted by Potiphar—only to be thrown into prison. We can be certain that through all of this, Joseph was sustained by the faith imparted in his dreams. He knew the end of the story.

Joseph's story contains many important lessons. We know all the promises of God are "yes" and "amen" (see II Corinthians 1:20). However, there is often a difficult walk of faith on the way to the fulfillment of such promises and dreams. Joseph's story also teaches us we should not expect our brothers to be as excited about our dreams of destiny as we are. Yet God has given us a tremendous gift in prophetic dreams. He knows the future, and He has decided to share it with us.

8

GENERATIONAL DREAMS

The Scriptures tell us that blessings and curses pass from one generation to another. As God was preparing Israel to enter the Promised Land and begin to live as His chosen people in the earth, He gave them this revelation:

> **I, the LORD your God, am a jealous**
> **God, visiting the iniquity of the fathers**
> **upon the children to the third and fourth**
> **generations of those who hate Me,**
>
> **but showing mercy to thousands, to those**
> **who love Me and keep My commandments**
> **(see Deuteronomy 5:9-10).**

It is clear from this and many similar passages that there are curses (and blessings) passed from generation to generation. This biblical principle has a profound application in dreams. In the previous chapter, we looked at prophetic dreams that foretell the future. Here we will explore generational dreams, which deal primarily with the past.

FROM GENERATION TO GENERATION

My father had blonde hair and blue eyes as a child. I had blonde hair and blue eyes as a child. My sons have blonde hair and blue eyes. Physical traits do not always pass from one generation to another, but they often do. This is because biological DNA is passed from one generation to another. Fathers and mothers literally pass a part of themselves to their children.

Similarly, I have fought some of the same battles in my personal and spiritual life that my father and grandfathers fought. I have also walked in some of the same gifting and blessing they walked in. This is because spiritual DNA passed from generation to generation that is as significant, if not more significant, than biological DNA.

Practically, this means the decisions and lifestyle of an individual affect not only their life, but also the lives of all who come after them. This realization should cause us to live soberly, with a vision for the next generation. We should take note that the iniquities are visited upon **"the third and fourth generations of those who hate** [God]." This implies that through repentance and restoration to the Lord, these curses may be broken by a generation who loves God. Second, the blessings of loving God are passed to a thousand generations, not just three or four (see Deuteronomy 7:9). This means that generational blessings are three hundred times more powerful than generational curses! We do not have to live under the curses of our parent's or grandparent's disobedience. We can live under the accumulated blessing of all the righteous acts of our ancestors—all the way back to Adam and Eve.

TAPPING INTO ANOTHER TIME

People commonly dream about family members of a previous generation, even those who have died. Sometimes these dreams take place in a home or setting remembered from childhood. They may illustrate a common theme in their family history, perhaps dysfunctional relationships, cluttered or chaotic households, or untrustworthy family members. The dreams may display positive scenes as well—an encouraging and comforting grandparent, a relative giving a gift, or they may emphasize the gifting or ministry of a forefather.

There are countless examples of this kind of dream, but in essence they see into another generation, recent or distant. These dreams often reveal generational blessings or curses. At times, they even accomplish something in the life of the dreamer, such as exposing and breaking the power of a curse or revealing and imparting a blessing. These generational dreams can be extremely useful. Once we are made aware of generational blessings and curses, we are able to respond appropriately. If we discover that an active curse has been passed through our bloodline, we can repent of any generational or personal iniquity and seek the Lord for restoration (more on this below). When we see that the favor of God or a particular blessing is in our family history, we can begin to appropriate this blessing and receive it into our own lives.

Generational dreams have been one of the most powerful means of inner healing in my life. For several years, I intermittently dreamed of my maternal and paternal grandparents. In one dream, I walked through a dark basement in the house of my grandparents' on one side. It was a scary, ominous scene. In another dream, I was in the attic of a house that my other grandfather and I were building. It was a beautiful, sunny day and my grandfather looked young and full of vitality.

In dreams, a basement may speak of several things. The basement may be the foundation that a life or family is built upon. It may also speak of a dark place where things are hidden or kept from the light of day. In my "basement dream," the Lord revealed to me things that had not been brought into the light and were hiding in the foundation of my family line. The dream ended with a fire burning down the walls of the basement, letting light shine in and freeing captives who were trapped inside.

An attic in dreams may also speak of several things—a high or heavenly place, the mind, or things forgotten. However, in my "attic dream," I was with my grandfather building a house. We were standing on top of the lower level and together we were building the attic, the top level. There was no roof or ceiling on the house, and we were still building. We were having a wonderful conversation, basking in the beautiful sunlight. This dream revealed godly heritage in my history that I am privileged to build upon. The ceiling of previous generations is my ground floor, and there is nowhere to go but up. I am building with the help of those who came before me. When I arrive at my ceiling, it will be the ground floor for my children and the generations to come.

During this season of dreams pertaining to my grandparents, not every dream had a conclusion like the two above. Some were merely illustrations of blessings or curses in my family line, and each one gave me more understanding of my heritage. In instances of blessing, I responded with thanksgiving to God, posturing myself in expectation to receive the blessing in my own life. In instances of curses or iniquity, I repented for every way that I had participated in these sins. I also repented on behalf of those who came before me and declared that the power of iniquity was broken. I then asked God for cleansing and victory for my family and generations to come. This process of identifying with previous generations and repenting on their behalf is called identificational repentance.

REPENTING AND APPROPRIATING

Identificational repentance for and receiving the blessings of previous generations are biblical responses. We see examples of both in the Book of Daniel and in the heritage of King David. In Daniel 9:2, Daniel reads the prophecy of Jeremiah, a righteous prophet who came before him. Jeremiah had prophesied that Israel would go into captivity because of their iniquity. However, after seventy years, God would deliver them. Daniel took it upon himself to respond to the iniquity of previous generations. Daniel confesses the sins of his ancestors as though he himself were guilty of them:

> And I prayed to the LORD my God, and
> made confession, and said, "O Lord, great
> and awesome God, who keeps His covenant

**and mercy with those who love Him, and
with those who keep His commandments,**

**we have sinned and committed iniquity,
we have done wickedly and rebelled, even
by departing from Your precepts and
Your judgments" (Daniel 9:4-5).**

Daniel was a righteous man, yet he repeatedly said, "We have sinned," as he identified with and repented for the iniquity of his ancestors. He then proceeded to ask God to remember His promise to restore Israel and Jerusalem.

Clearly, the effects of generational iniquity were at work in David's life. In Psalm 51:5 he says to God, **"I was brought forth in iniquity."** Aside from being a descendant of Adam, David was a descendant of Rahab the harlot. We know that sexual immorality was David's downfall and it brought devastation to his descendants. David's son, Amnon, raped his daughter, Tamar. David's son, Absalom, then murdered Amnon and usurped David's throne, even having sex with David's concubines in the sight of all Israel (see II Samuel 16:22). Eventually, immorality also caused David's son, Solomon, to turn from the true God.

Regardless of these tragedies of generational iniquity, tremendous generational blessings resulted from David's life of worship and intimacy with God. Over and over in the Scriptures, we see God doing things **"for the sake of My servant David" (see I Kings 11; II Kings 19:34; Hosea 3:5).** Hundreds of years after David died, God spoke to Isaiah that He would save Jerusalem for the sake of David. We also see that for generations Israel would call out to God as they ascended Mount Zion asking Him to bless them **"for David's sake" (see Psalm 132)**. They were appropriating the blessings in their bloodline because of David. David was a man in his generation who loved God (see Deuteronomy 7:9), therefore passing blessings to his progeny. May we all pursue lives that will perpetuate blessing and favor from God "to a thousand generations."

GENERATIONAL REDEMPTION

This season of dreams about my grandparents culminated in a powerful dream. I was with one of my grandfathers on his property. He is the pastor of a fundamentalist Baptist church and several of his parishioners were with us, waiting to speak to him. I began to weep as I stood before him. I hugged and kissed him, and with my heart overflowing with affection, between sobs I said over and over, "Thank you for preaching the Gospel. I honor you for preaching the Gospel." This was a beautiful ending to a season of generational restoration. In spite of the imperfections of my forefathers, I have obtained the blessing of God that was on their lives. I have received a generational blessing and anointing from those who walked with God in my family line.

Since then, I have dreamed of both of my parents. The Lord is walking me through a similar process of redemption, one generation down the line. Our dreams are a powerful means of seeing the unseen, even invisible curses and blessings in our heritage. Generational dreams free us from the past and bless us into the future.

9

SOULISH DREAMS

In the previous chapter, we explored generational dreams. We will now endeavor to understand dreams from the soul, a common experience in the night.

The soul has often been described as the mind, will, and emotions. The New Testament word for soul, *psuche*, refers to a person's inner life. Some dreams come from our soul, rather than from the Lord. As we discussed previously, dreams often allow us to see things we may miss while awake. When we sleep, it is as though the distractions of our "carnal nature" are put aside and we are able to accurately perceive what is transpiring in our souls.

Life can be difficult. Even those who live in pursuit of God traverse a path often marked by problems and pain. As we work through this difficulty and pain, we sometimes develop defense mechanisms, subconscious attempts to protect ourselves. We may even deceive ourselves into thinking our hearts are healthy when in reality they are not (see I John 1:8). Deception of the heart is the dilemma of living according to the natural order, or "the flesh" (see Jeremiah 17:9). This is one reason we are constantly exhorted to walk in the Spirit—not the flesh (see Galatians 5:16 and Romans 8:5). Soulish dreams can be helpful in revealing unresolved issues in our souls, providing us the opportunity to receive healing from God.

DREAMING OF "THE WAY THINGS USED TO BE...."

At times we dream of things we used to do in our "old life" before we came to Christ. We may dream of partying or sleeping around, things that we now consider sinful and repulsive. Sometimes these dreams come because we have encountered a person living an ungodly lifestyle or we visited a place with an unholy atmosphere. Our spirit may have felt the influence of this person or atmosphere, and our soul remembers our old lifestyle in the dream. However, in other instances, especially if these dreams are recurring, there could be a deeper issue.

If we begin to regularly dream of partaking in sin that the Lord has already freed us from, it may indicate that we are engaging in something that is re-awakening or stimulating our old nature. Even though we have not returned to a life of immorality or drunkenness, we may be indulging the flesh, spending time with the wrong people, or even watching television shows that stimulate our carnal nature. It may also be that we are beginning to slip in areas of devotion or discipline and our soul begins to move in a detrimental direction. We must remember Galatians 6:8:

> He who sows to his flesh will of the flesh reap corruption, but he who sows to the Spirit will of the Spirit reap everlasting life.

These soulish dreams serve as helpful warnings that we are headed down a path leading to a bad place. However, they are not always a warning from the Lord as much as an alarm going off in our soul when we begin to lean towards sin. This kind of dream expounds upon what transpires in our inner life.

FREUD'S INSIGHTS AND INCONSISTENCIES

Many consider Sigmund Freud to be a pioneer in dream interpretation theory. Freudian theory was based on the idea of "repression." He believed that humans repress certain thoughts or memories by blocking them out of the conscious mind. He taught that dreams were an outlet for the subconscious to release those repressed thoughts and feelings.

Much of Freud's psychological theory was based on the idea that when life issues are too embarrassing, painful, or difficult to process, people hide them. That is where supposed "Freudian slips" come into play. These repressed thoughts, memories, and feelings slip out into conversation when we least expect it.

There is some truth to Freud's ideas of repression and the subconscious. Most of us hide in some way, just like our father Adam "hid" behind the fig leaf. Dreams from the soul can be an outlet that forces us to acknowledge fear or shame working in some deep place in our hearts. However, where Freud's interpretation theory, indeed his whole psychological framework, falls apart is in his denial of human sin.

We repress things because we have sinned or have been sinned against. Dealing with this reality is painful. We have deceived ourselves (see I John 1:8) into believing that there is no shame or pain. Therefore, dreams from the soul, which reveal issues in our hearts, can be useful. Dreams can show us exactly which areas of our lives need healing, repentance, or forgiveness.

GOING DEEP AT THE COFFEE SHOP

Several years ago, I taught a class on prophetic evangelism at the Forerunner School of Ministry in Kansas City. I gave each of my students an assignment to set up some sort of outreach during the semester. One of them obtained permission to set up a dream interpretation table at a local coffee shop.

It is surprisingly easy to do this sort of outreach, especially if the coffee shop is a small, privately owned business. If you explain that you and some friends will purchase drinks and you would like to set a sign on the table that says "Free Dream Interpretation," the owner will typically allow you to.

On this particular day, a couple of students and I ordered drinks and set a "Free Dream Interpretation" sign on our table. It started out slowly, but we had a great time fellowshipping together. There was a young man sitting alone at the table next to us. We'll call him Jason. We invited Jason over for a free dream interpretation and he gladly accepted. He told us of a recurring dream he'd had since he was a young boy.

Some recurring dreams are from the Lord, but many are from the soul. For instance, if someone dreams again and again of being laughed at by people whom they want to be accepted by, their soul is likely in need of healing. In this case, they probably have issues with rejection or fear of man. The blessing of this kind of dream is that the issues are exposed in our souls, enabling us to deal with them. Dreams can be an accurate discerner of the soul.

In Jason's recurring dream, he was swimming in the pool behind his childhood home. Suddenly, he lost his footing and began to drown. He was flailing and gasping for breath, and all the while his father stood next to the pool watching him. Jason's father could have easily reached in and saved him, but he chose not to. Jason said that in the dream he always thought to himself, "I'm drowning. Why won't my dad help me?" Then he would wake up.

This dream was clearly related to a wound in Jason's heart regarding his father. I asked him if anything had happened in his relationship with his dad around the time he began having the dream. Often, this sort of question is useful in determining the source of a soulish dream. He said, "Yes, that was about the time my parents divorced. From that time forward, my dad was not around much."

I explained to Jason that the dream reflected a wounded place in his soul. As he grew up, at certain times, when it seemed like life was too much, he needed his father to be there for him, to keep him from drowning. Since his dad was not around, it felt as though he was flailing and gasping for breath, looking for someone to help him out—but his father was nowhere to be found.

As I explained this, Jason held his head down and began to cry. The interpretation was obviously accurate and a door was wide open for ministry. I explained that the only way for this wound to be healed was for Jason to forgive his dad for hurting him.

As I talked about the process of forgiveness, we discovered that Jason was a Christian. He said he was willing to forgive his dad, and we led him through a simple prayer. When we were finished, this nineteen-year-old young man, who had cried in a public place for forty-five minutes, had received deep ministry and had forgiven and blessed his father.

We only interpreted dreams for a few people that day, and I do not remember any of the others. I will never forget, however, the way God powerfully met this young man in the middle of a coffee shop and changed his life forever. All because a few believers bought some lattes and set a sign on their table.

Just because a dream is from the human soul rather than from God does not mean it is without purpose. We are **"fearfully and wonderfully made" (see Psalm 139:14)** and God has designed every part of us, including our soul, to bring Him glory. Let us address our souls like the Psalmist, **"Why are you cast down, O my soul? And why are you disquieted within me? Hope in God; for I shall yet praise Him, the help of my countenance and my God" (Psalm 42:11).** We will function at our highest potential when our soul is healed and praising God. He is the One who heals and helps our countenance.

10

INTERCESSION AND SPIRITUAL WARFARE DREAMS

s it possible to pray **"always with all prayer and supplication in the Spirit" (see Ephesians 6:18)**? This verse, included in the significant section on spiritual warfare and the armor of God in Ephesians 6, encourages continual communion with God, calling us to live a life of prayer in every situation. Is it possible to pray even when we sleep?

Our dreams often accomplish intercession. Many dreams are not merely about intercession, they are intercession. Several years ago, I helped create a powerful prophetic evangelism ministry as part of a remarkable church. They had an ongoing evangelistic outreach and a dynamic prophetic ministry, but the two had not yet joined to take the prophetic gifts to the streets.

We began setting up tables to do dream interpretation and prophetic ministry, which we called "destiny words" or "spiritual readings." We did this in many settings, such as art festivals, community events, and even psychic fairs. We utilized the gifts of the Spirit to impact people and prepare their hearts to hear the Gospel. Miracles, deliverance, and salvations happened every time we went to an event.

Several months after launching the ministry, I dreamed I was at a large festival with two friends, one gifted in evangelism and the other in the prophetic. In the dream, we moved through the crowd ministering. One friend would prophesy to someone and their heart would open to receive the Lord. I then wept and groaned in travailing intercession for their soul (see Galatians 4:19 KJV). Finally, I introduced the person to my other friend who preached the Gospel to them.

In the dream, God affirmed our prophetic evangelism strategy, which Jesus Himself often used (see John 1:45–51 and John 4:7–26). However, there was more to the dream. My travailing intercession felt real. The experience of prayer in my dream was more powerful than anything I experienced while awake. I woke up knowing that my spirit man was accomplishing powerful work in the spiritual realm while I was asleep. The dream was not merely about intercession, it was intercession. We had prayed for the evangelism ministry for months, and my spirit decided to "pray continually," even while I slept.

During the following season of prayer and evangelism, we saw remarkable things happen. Our outreach to the New Age, under the moniker "The Mystics of Yeshua," saw significant fruit. Billing ourselves as "mystics" who listened to the Spirit of Yeshua and spoke His word, we explained that we broke darkness off of people's lives and released light to their soul. In short, we prophesied to people and prayed for them. We also shared the Gospel to these new-agers and saw salvations, healings, deliverance, and even baptisms in the Spirit.

Although eventually discovered as a Christian group and banned from future events, we had nevertheless become the most popular attraction at the Psychical Research Society's fairs. Lines of people waited to receive from us. The fair organizers began sending attendees to us, telling them "The Mystics of Yeshua have the hottest energy in the whole reading room!" Two witches who made a living at these events even renounced witchcraft and came to Christ. One of them saw a team member at a house church meeting several years later and told him, "You may not remember me, but you shared Jesus with me while I was fortune telling at a psychic fair. God used that to bring me to salvation!"

WRESTLING WITH POWERS AND PRINCIPALITIES

In 2007, I attended a Joseph Company Summit in Kansas City where Rick Joyner was the keynote speaker. At the beginning of a morning session, Rick shared an experience from the night before: "I didn't sleep well last night. I was wrestling with a principality over Kansas City. I am not sure exactly what it was, but it felt sophisticated, like organized crime. I sometimes have this kind of encounter when I travel. It's just part of my calling." This caught my attention. Rick had not merely had a dream— he had engaged in spiritual warfare over the city.

During 2007 and 2008, an intricate network of organized crime in Kansas City began to unravel. Authorities busted an immense human trafficking network with three hundred forty-one prostitution related arrests in 2007 and more in 2008. Rick's experience in spiritual warfare joined with the prayers of the saints for the defeat of evil in the city. His dream was not merely about spiritual warfare—it was spiritual warfare.

While interpreting dreams for Christians over the past decade, I discovered that intercession dreams and spiritual warfare dreams are quite common. Many times these dreams manifest as epic battle scenes with supernatural imagery and physics-defying feats, like scenes from *The Matrix*. Believers, including myself, have dreamed of casting demons out of people or fighting with someone who morphs into a demonic being. Some are deliverance dreams that set someone free. Sometimes the dreamer himself is delivered. In real-life deliverance ministry, you can feel the battle waging and sense when a spirit leaves. The experience of the battle and the victory can be just as real in spiritual warfare dreams.

MORE REAL THAN YOU REALIZE

Intercession dreams are powerful because the prayers of the saints are potent in spiritual warfare. When Daniel began his twenty-one days of fasting and prayer, war exploded in the heavens. Michael the Archangel was the prince (or principality) standing guard in the heavenly realm over Israel (see Daniel 12:1). There was also an evil principality in the heavens over Babylon and Persia, the Prince of Persia (see Daniel 10:13). When Daniel fasted and prayed for Israel, God dispatched an angel (likely

Gabriel) to confront the Prince of Persia. Soon joined by Michael, the two withstood the demonic principality.

Daniel was unaware that this war took place in concert with his prayer. Gabriel appeared to Daniel and explained that from the first day of his fast, heaven responded in power. Nothing in Daniel's experience alerted him to the magnitude of his prayer's impact. Gabriel essentially said to him, "Daniel, you do not fully appreciate who you are. You are greatly beloved in heaven and are a man of great authority. Your weakness in these twenty-one days of fasting and prayer shifted heavenly dominions and changed history!" (see Daniel 10)

Just as Daniel needed encouragement as to the power of his intercession, we must understand the significance of the warfare and intercession in our dreams that sometimes shifts the heavens and changes history. Some of these dreams win victories for those we know and others for people we will never meet in this life. Battles fought in our dreams are more real than we realize.

My wife often tells me that she is awakened in the night by me praying in tongues as I sleep. On a couple occasions, she awakened to me sitting up in the bed and pointing at and rebuking invisible things. I have even awakened both of us by shaking in the bed in travailing prayer in a dream. I have no recollection of these experiences the next morning. Such experiences are powerful manifestations of intercession and spiritual warfare.

LeeAnna and I once interpreted dreams for a small group of believers. One after another they shared dreams in which they confronted or cast out demons. They were encouraged to learn they were fighting and prevailing in spiritual battles as they slept. I quickly realized this small band of warriors was waging war and winning battles for their city, church, and family.

In Scripture, the Lord referred to Himself as the "Lord of Hosts," or literally the "Lord of Armies," more than any other name. If we live as we are called to, we have enlisted ourselves in the Lord's army and fight His battles. Warfare is a normal part of the Christian life. If we wage war while awake, it should not be surprising that our spirit wages war while we sleep.

11

SPIRITUAL ATTACK DREAMS

Some experiences in the night are demonically inspired, coming from the realm of darkness as a spiritual attack. This category includes nightmares and sexually perverted dreams. Discerning this type of dream is not difficult. If a dream imparts the fear of death or evil, it is not from God. **"God has not given us a spirit of fear, but of power and of love and of a sound mind" (see II Timothy 1:7;** also Hebrews 4:15). Further, dreams awakening lust or a desire for immorality are clearly a spiritual attack since we called to "flee immorality," letting not "even a hint" of it exist in us (see I Corinthians 6:18 and Ephesians 5:3).

The Scriptures include different categories of demons. Ephesians 6 reveals a hierarchy in the kingdom of darkness. We see spiritual forces called principalities, powers, rulers of the darkness of this world, and spiritual wickedness in high places. It seems that these various "ranks" of spirits operate at different levels, some influencing culture and world events, others attacking individuals. The previous chapter explored the realm of warfare in the heavens. In this chapter, we will examine demonic attacks on individuals through dreams.

The Bible teaches that various evil spirits have specific demonic powers. For instance, in Luke 13:11 we find **"a woman who had a spirit of infirmity eighteen years, and was bent over and could in no way raise herself up."** A demon that caused physical infirmity tormented this woman. Jesus delivered her of the demon and she was healed. We also see New Testament examples of spirits of fear (see II Timothy 1:7), impurity (see Matthew 12:3), divination (see Acts 16:16), deaf and dumb spirits (see Mark 9:25), antichrist (see I John 4:3), and many others.

CHEAP SHOTS, ILLEGAL TRESPASSES, AND OPEN DOORS

A spiritual attack dream occurs when a demonic spirit attacks or influences someone in his or her sleep. If a spirit of fear assaults a person, they may have terrifying nightmares. If an impure spirit or spirit of lust attacks, a person may dream of sexually perverted scenes. Upon waking from such a dream, the individual may still feel the evil spirit's influence. Perhaps the emotional experience of fear persists and they remain unsettled throughout the day. Or the immoral images and emotions have stirred unwelcomed sexual desire. To use imagery from Rick Joyner's book, *The Final Quest*, these spirits have "slimed" the person and they need cleansing of the evil influence.

A spiritual attack dream is not necessarily an indication that we have sinned or participated with evil. Often these dreams come as an illegal trespass. The enemy takes "cheap shots" any way he can. He is deceptive and does not fight fair. At times he tries to plant evil thoughts and feelings into our souls as we dream. In some cases, however, these dreams may reveal that the enemy has an open door of access into our life. Especially in the case of recurring spiritual attack dreams, we should seek revelation from the Holy Spirit, asking if we have opened a door to them. Dreams with a recurring demonic theme can highlight areas where repentance or another response is needed.

For example, if someone grew up in an abusive home and now repeatedly has terrifying dreams about his or her childhood, there could be a door open to the spirit of fear. The person may need deliverance or inner healing, or they may need to forgive the abuser and renounce the fearful memories. If someone has engaged in immoral sinful activity or pornography in the past and now has sexual dreams, repentance is needed to shut the door of access to these attacks.

After teaching on dreams at a Bible school, I had a student share a terrifying experience she had the previous night. She vividly dreamed of wrestling with Satan, to the point of being destroyed by him at any moment. Still disturbed and shaken, she explained that the experience seemed so real that she physically felt the battle. I asked her if she had recently been exposed to anything demonic that may have given access to this attack. She confessed to having watched a popular vampire movie before going to bed the previous night. By watching such a film, she had opened herself to this attack. She repented and renounced the movie as we prayed together. She was immediately set free from the dream's lingering oppression.

Shutting the door on spiritual attack dreams may be as simple as renouncing a movie we have watched or a conversation in which we participated. By repentance and renunciation, we close the access points for demonic attack.

FLUSHING AWAY DEFILEMENT

Though a spiritual attack dream may reveal where the enemy has access, they do not deserve serious reflection. Interpreting a demonically inspired dream is pointless as the only message is from the devil. We do not want to waste time pondering his plans for our lives. Rather, we want to "flush" away the defilement of these dreams, severing them from our souls.

As stated above, upon waking up from a spiritual attack dream, we may still feel its influence. If we wake up feeling fear, shame, lust, or other ungodly emotions, it is important to go through a cleansing process. God plants seeds within us that grow into good works and the fruit of the Holy Spirit, but the enemy also seeks to plant his seed in us. Just as God may impart faith through an epic destiny dream (see chapter 7, Prophetic Dreams), demonic powers like to impart fear to our soul.

When I wake up from this kind of dream, I immediately bring it before the Lord, renouncing the dream and all of its images and emotions. I ask the Lord to remove any seed the enemy has planted in me and to reveal ways I may have opened a door to it. If repentance or forgiveness is needed, I take advantage of the opportunity to get right with God. At times, it is helpful to have someone to agree with you to break the dream's power. When my wife or I have this sort of dream, we pray with one another like this: "Lord we come before Your throne to receive cleansing from this dream. We renounce all the thoughts, emotions, and images from the dream and cut them off from our souls. We break the power of any demonic influence and we bind this spirit from attacking us any longer. Jesus, we set our minds on things above and we choose to dwell on Your righteous plan for our lives." This is the process of "flushing" our system after a spiritual attack dream.

CONSECRATING THE NIGHT SEASON

The average person sleeps for one third of their life. In light of this, it is wise to consecrate our sleep to the Lord each night by asking God to speak to us in dreams and protect our sleep from demonic attack. We may also need to take authority over any evil spirits that have recently attacked our dreams.

There is **"A time of war, and a time of peace" (see Ecclesiastes 3:8).** Certain seasons come with intensified warfare and we need to respond offensively, taking the initiative in the battle. Some activities, such as deliverance ministry or focused intercession, are accompanied by greater spiritual warfare and we would do well to prepare ourselves. During these times of intensified warfare, we can rest in peace, knowing the One in us is greater than all the demonic forces in the world (see I John 4:3–5).

12

VISITATION DREAMS

The Bible records many instances of God visiting people in dreams. In the Book of Genesis alone, we see Him visiting Abimelech, Jacob, and Laban in this way.

Perhaps the most remarkable visitation of God in a dream is found in I Kings 2:5–15. Solomon was at Gibeon to offer a sacrifice and the Lord appeared to him at night in his sleep. God practically gave him a blank check saying, "Ask! What shall I give you?" Solomon asked for an understanding heart and discernment. God promised to answer this request and also to give him riches and honor. As the story unfolded we saw each of these qualities manifest abundantly in Solomon's life.

Throughout Scripture we find another phenomenon—angels visiting people in dreams to bring the word of the Lord. Daniel, Joseph (the father of Jesus), the Apostle Paul, and others experienced this kind of visitation. Angels are involved in many revelatory experiences, especially those in which we receive a message. The Hebrew and Greek words for "angel" both literally mean "messenger."

The writer of Hebrews tells us that many have encountered angels without realizing it (see Hebrews 13:2). In context, Hebrews describes instances of angels coming in human form. Sometimes the human messenger speaking to us in a dream is actually an angel.

There are innumerable present-day examples of God and angels visiting people in dreams. God is the same yesterday, today, and forever (see Hebrews 13:8) and we should expect Him to visit people in this way today, as He always has. I have been amazed in recent years by the stories I have heard of Muslims in closed nations coming to faith in Jesus after being visited by Him in dreams. Some missionaries associated with MorningStar reported visiting secluded villages, places where the occupants have never heard the Gospel, to discover the villagers dreamed of Jesus. As the preachers shared the Gospel, villagers replied, "We know whom you are speaking of. This is 'the man in white' who has come to many of us in dreams. Now we know His name!" The Lord had sown seeds in the harvest fields and these missionaries were blessed to reap the fruit.

JESUS IS THE GREAT EVANGELIST

This phenomenon of divine visitation in dreams is especially prevalent in Iran. One MorningStar missionary, who works with the underground church in Iran, estimates that over 3,000,000 Iranian have come to Christ in recent years through a visitation of Jesus in a dream or vision.

An Iranian woman (who wishes to remain anonymous for the safety of her family still living in Iran) recently shared with me stories of how she and many of her friends accepted Jesus. We will call her Hadis.

Hadis was raised as a Muslim, and thus spiritual dreams were important to her. In 2010, she dreamed of a man dressed in white with a white beard and white hair, although He was not old. In the presence of this man, she could not keep from weeping. She asked Him if the many terrible things she experienced in life were because of witchcraft being used against her. He answered, "No, it's not because of witchcraft, but you must now make an important decision." She woke up shaken by the dream, not fully understanding it.

The following week she dreamed that she accompanied a co-worker to church. When they arrived, the door was shut and a long line of people waited outside. A woman stepped out from a door at the top of a stairway and pointed to Hadis, inviting her to come inside. Hadis did not know if her co-worker was a Christian in real life, but shortly after having this dream, she asked her. The woman confessed to being a Christian and invited Hadis to come to church. There, Hadis heard the Gospel and realized the man in her dream was Jesus. He was calling her to decide to follow Him as Lord. She joyfully accepted His invitation.

Several of Hadis' friends also came to Christ through dreams. One dreamed of opening a door to find a prophet standing in front of her. She knew it was the prophet Jesus and not Muhammad because He looked so kind. Jesus handed her a book and said, "This is the truth." He then extended to her a tray of bread and wine and said, "This is for you." She answered, "Oh no, I can't take that! I'm a Muslim." He smiled and said, "Yes, I know. But this is for you." Then the dream ended.

A rumor in this Iranian community said that a certain pastor's wife could interpret dreams. Hadis' friend went to the pastor's wife and received the dream's interpretation. She understood that Jesus was offering her eternal life and gladly accepted Him as Savior.

Another of Hadis' Iranian friends met some Christians in Turkey and became curious about Jesus. Some family members sent her a box of books about "religion," saying they would be helpful in her quest for truth. Uninterested in other religions, she did not open the box. Instead, she prayed for three days that if Jesus was the true God, He would show Himself to her. At the end of the three days, she had a dream.

In this dream, Jesus placed a hand on her shoulder and said, "What are you looking for? I love you and I know your heart is broken. From the time you were born, I have been with you—in your sadness and your happiness. Do you want to see Me? Go and open the box of books you were given." She immediately woke up and opened the box. On top was a book with a picture of Jesus on the cover called, *The Jesus I Never Knew*. The other books were also about Christianity. That day, she trusted in Jesus for salvation and was baptized in a river the next morning.

In researching this phenomenon, I discovered dozens of similar testimonies. It seems that God Himself is answering the age-old question, "What about those who have never had the opportunity to hear the Gospel?" He is personally evangelizing and revealing Himself to many in closed, persecuted countries.

VISITATIONS OF ANOTHER SORT

Scriptures reveal another sort of supernatural visitation. In Acts 16, Paul and his companions struggled to determine the will of God. They endeavored to go into new regions to preach the Gospel, yet were "forbidden" by the Spirit of Jesus to do so. They did not know what to do next, until one night **"A vision appeared to Paul in the night. A man of Macedonia stood and pleaded with him, saying, 'Come over to Macedonia and help us'" (Acts 16:9).** Paul was immediately obedient to this vision, and he and his companions traveled to Macedonia to preach the Gospel.

Who was the man in the dream or night vision? Other places in the New Testament specify when an angel visits someone, so the man in Paul's nighttime experience was probably not an angel. Some have suggested that this was a visitation of Jesus in another form. However, again the Bible is often explicit when Jesus visits someone. Is it possible that a living, breathing "man of Macedonia" appeared to Paul and pleaded with him to come?

In Scripture, there are other instances of humans supernaturally visiting people. In several places, those who had died returned to speak with someone who was still living. These include Samuel in I Samuel 28:1–19 and Moses and Elijah in Matthew 17:1–3. Further, mysterious passages like I Corinthians 5:3 tell us Paul was "present" at a church discipline meeting in Corinth even though he was physically in Ephesus, on the other side of the Aegean Sea. He traveled to Corinth not physically, but in the Spirit.

Again in Colossians 2:5, Paul writes, **"For though I am absent in the flesh, yet I am with you in spirit, rejoicing to see your good order and the steadfastness of your faith in Christ."** He had never visited the church in Colossae and wrote from a prison in Rome, over nine hundred miles away. However, he had seen their good order and steadfast faith by visiting them "in spirit." Finally, several passages speak of someone being physically translated from one place to another, such as Acts 8:39–40. God whisked Philip away to preach to the people of Azotus after baptizing the Ethiopian eunuch.

The principle mentioned above from Hebrews 13:8, that God is the same yesterday, today, and forever, is also relevant here. If someone could be supernaturally translated or travel in the Spirit in biblical times, it is possible today. It was extraordinary two thousand years ago when a man from Macedonia visited Paul in a dream to give him a message. This extraordinary phenomenon still occurs today.

WHO WAS THAT MAN?

At the end of a long season of wrestling with God, I had a dream. I had felt convicted to make a significant lifestyle change, but I could not understand why God would require this of me. I procrastinated in obeying God for a long time until my dream unequivocally confirmed what He was saying.

I dreamed of standing at a crossroad. A strong African man stood, holding a familiar book in front of me. It was a journal that I kept during two years of unparalleled intimacy and encounter with God. The pages of this journal were filled with the testimony of the life I was created for. The man's deep voice spoke with a thick accent, "What was it like to live like this?"

I remembered what it was like—it was awesome! I longed for the intimacy with God and supernatural exploits I had experienced. As I pondered the man's question, he spoke again in his powerful voice: "God has told you many times to make this lifestyle change."

I awoke with the fear of God. I understood the implication of the dream. Because I had disobeyed God's directive, I was no longer experiencing the same high level of supernatural encounter with Him. I was at a "crossroad" in my dream because the Lord was calling me to walk the path of the cross. Death to my flesh would result in resurrection.

Over the course of the next year, I made the change the Lord had called me to. It was not easy, but in the process I was healed of a significant physical affliction. The Lord called me to change because, among other reasons, it would bring healing to my body. God's will is always the best thing for us, even when we do not understand it.

I learned a lot about obedience and the goodness of God from the experience. I also feel that the Lord showed me something about the man in my dream. He was a real person from somewhere in Africa, not just a vision. God spoke to me about making a lifestyle change and I was not listening. This man in Africa, however, was listening intently to God and walking in obedience. He had the same attitude as Isaiah, **"Here am I! Send me" (see Isaiah 6:8).** The Lord gave him a word for me and allowed him to appear in my dream to give the message, even though I was thousands of miles away.

Dreams are a mysterious and glorious gift from God. Not only can we receive important information in them, but they can also be a vehicle of visitation from angels, people, and even God Himself.

13

WARNING DREAMS

"**I am innocent of the blood of this just Person**" (see Matthew 27:24). Pilate's noble claim echoes in our ears two thousand years after the cross. If only it were true. Pilate had been convicted by his conscience, as the Gospel of John clearly portrayed (see 18:33–19:22). He was explicitly warned through his wife's dream: "**While he was sitting on the judgment seat, his wife sent to him, saying, 'Have nothing to do with that just Man, for I have suffered many things today in a dream because of Him'**" (Matthew 27:19). Pilate had been thoroughly warned and was far from innocent. How many warning dreams have likewise gone unheeded in history?

We previously examined several biblical examples of warning dreams. Joseph, the father of Jesus, adhered to dreams from God to save His Son, and the Magi followed dreams to foil Herod's wrath (see Matthew chapters 1 and 2). In Genesis 20, Abimelech heeded the voice of God in his dream and realm-wide calamity was averted. Job highlights warnings as a basic function of dreams, **"In a dream, in a vision of the night, when deep sleep falls upon men . . . [God] opens the ears of men . . . In order to turn man from his deed . . . He keeps back his soul from the Pit, and his life from perishing by the sword"** (see Job 33:15–18). Warnings in dreams are meant to turn us from certain deeds, to save our soul from the pit, and to keep us from perishing.

God is merciful and He takes no pleasure in a person's calamity (see Ezekiel 33:11 and 18:23). In Genesis, God gave a warning before He destroyed Sodom and Gomorrah. In Exodus, He warned Pharaoh before He poured out each judgment on Egypt. The entire Book of Jonah tells the story of the relentless measures God will take to communicate a warning. Indeed, many of the literary prophets warned wicked nations in great detail of impending judgment, giving them opportunity to change course. Warning dreams are a revelation of the nature of God. He is good. He loves to rescue, to redeem. He is the Savior.

OFFERING A WAY OUT

Matt was my best friend in high school. Unfortunately, I introduced him to the dark world of dealing drugs and he thrived in it. Once I became a Christian, Matt was my primary target for evangelism. The only problem was that he did not want to talk about God, Jesus, or religion. Since my efforts were fruitless, I prayed fervently that God would speak to Matt in dreams.

We met for lunch one afternoon, but despite my efforts, I got nowhere in ministering to him. However, when we started to leave, Matt said, "I've been having a recurring dream I want to ask you about. I dream of being in a large room filled with smoke. I desperately want to leave but as I aimlessly feel around, I cannot find the door. What do you think it means?"

This dream was too easy to interpret. I explained, "This is a dream from God. The room you are stuck in is the lifestyle you are living—selling drugs and partying. These things have blinded you from seeing the way out, that's why the room was full of smoke. There is a way out—it's Jesus. He is the door and He will set you free from these things you are trapped in."

Matt explained that he thought that's what the dream meant and I noticed he had tears in his eyes. Matt was the toughest guy I knew. Fearless and always ready for a fight, he had broken several bones in his hands on various people's heads. He was raised in a bad neighborhood, in a difficult family situation, and was exposed to drugs and alcohol from a young age. Suffice it to say, it was not Matt's custom to cry.

I asked him, "What do you think, do you want to walk through the door with Jesus? He'll save you and set you free. Are you ready to commit your life to Him? I'll walk with you and support you in every way I can." After a moment's hesitation, Matt shook his head and said he was not ready to make such a commitment. We hugged and parted ways.

A couple days later, FBI agents knocked at Matt's door with a warrant for his arrest. A "friend" set him up as part of a plea bargain. They wore a wire in several drug deals with Matt and taped him negotiating the sale of large quantities of Ecstasy. He was charged with felony trafficking of narcotics and sentenced to ten years in prison. Matt ended up serving one year in prison, six months of house arrest, and two years of probation.

I believe Matt's dream and our ensuing conversation were God's offer of mercy before judgment. God can change impossible situations. I have seen people convicted of serious crimes serve no time in prison and it may be that God mercifully offered Matt an alternative outcome.

While Matt was in prison, we wrote each other on a regular basis. He started to read the Bible and began to turn toward the Lord. Within a few months, we were exchanging prayer requests and doing Bible studies together via letters. The season was a significant time of soul-searching for Matt, but unfortunately he has not yet accepted Jesus as Lord. Matt was recently arrested on drug charges again and is back in prison. We write each other and I continue to pray that he will walk through the Door.

HEAVEN'S HEADS UP

Some warning dreams are a "heads up" from heaven about what is coming, rather than a warning of imminent judgment. They prepare us for the future or inform us of new information. This is what happened in Genesis 41 when Pharaoh dreamed of cows and wheat. God wanted Egypt to prepare in the time of abundance for the impending famine. This is, of course, because God loved the Egyptians—but even more so because they would preserve His people, the sons of Israel, during the famine. If we will heed this kind of warning, we can posture ourselves to face impending difficulty.

A member of my family began to repeatedly dream that she lost the large diamond in her wedding ring. Several months after the dreams began she lost this diamond in real life. Around the same time, I dreamed of camping with her and others in the family. As we sat around the campfire, a minister we knew came and told us that a terrible storm was coming and our tents would not be sufficient shelter. We were alerted by this and went in search of better shelter.

The next morning, before I had time to interpret the dream, I received a phone call. My relative had uncovered her husband's extra-marital affair. The commitment in the marriage, which the diamond represented, had been lost. This infidelity unleashed a yearlong storm upon our family. The "tents," or our flesh (see II Corinthians 5:14), were not sufficient shelter in this storm. We had to press into the Lord as our shelter like never before.

My relative responded to this tragedy with whole-hearted devotion to the Lord. She immediately stepped into another level of faith and pursuit of God. Within two years, the Lord brought her a godly husband and they now have two children. They are successful business owners and have been in ministry together for most of the past ten years. When I asked her permission to share this story she answered emphatically, "Yes, but be sure to tell them that

God is a Redeemer! He brought restoration and blessed me beyond my greatest dreams. My life is a testimony of the goodness of God!"

God warns in dreams because He is compassionate—His nature overflows with mercy and redemption. May we respond wholeheartedly to His warning dreams.

14

SOMETHING MORE
THAN A DREAM

Jacob's life was supernatural. He was man with significant character flaws—and a remarkable relationship with the Lord. A cursory glance at Jacob's life reveals interaction with angels and visitations of God, extraordinary supernatural experiences. One of the most extraordinary was his encounter while sleeping at Bethel:

> So he came to a certain place and stayed there all night, because the sun had set. And he took one of the stones of that place and put it at his head, and he lay down in that place to sleep.

> Then he dreamed, and behold, a ladder was set up on the earth, and its top reached to heaven; and there the angels of God were ascending and descending on it.

> And behold, the LORD stood above it and said: "I am the LORD God of Abraham your father and the God of Isaac; the land on which you lie I will give to you and your descendants.

"Also your descendants shall be as the dust
of the earth; you shall spread abroad to
the west and the east, to the north and the
south; and in you and in your seed all the
families of the earth shall be blessed.

"Behold, I am with you and will keep you
wherever you go, and will bring you back
to this land; for I will not leave you until I
have done what I have spoken to you."

Then Jacob awoke from his sleep and said, "Surely
the LORD is in this place, and I did not know it."

And he was afraid and said, "How awesome is this
place! This is none other than the house of God,
and this is the gate of heaven!" (Genesis 28:11-17)

This scene from Jacob's life reveals a fascinating category of spiritual experience. Some dreams are real. The Scriptures imply that Jacob encountered a geographical location where a gate opened from heaven into the earth. Five times in Genesis 28:11–17 **"the place"** is emphasized, highlighting the significance of this locale. In the invisible realm, there was a palpable manifestation of heaven into the earth. When Jacob fell asleep, he passed through the "gate of heaven" into the house of God. Upon waking, he exclaimed, **"Surely the Lord is in this place, and I did not know it!"** An awesome dream did not amaze him—he was in awe of the fact that he had encountered angels and God Himself.

Examples in Scripture and in church history show people having experiences during sleep that are much more than a dream, such as another remarkable incident from Jacob's life in Genesis 32. Jacob, greatly distressed, is on his way to meet Esau. After an intense day of meeting a company of angels in the morning and sending delegations to appease Esau throughout the afternoon, he lay down to sleep in the evening. God came to Jacob in the form of a man and wrestled with him all night. By the break of day, Jacob had been blessed, had his hip dislocated, and his name changed to Israel. Although this experience happened during the night, this was clearly not a dream. Jacob experienced something real—forever changing his name and his walk.

The Bible reveals other encounters in the night that are "something more" than a dream. In Acts 27, Paul is aboard a ship seemingly doomed to destruction. In the middle of the night, an angel of the Lord stood by Paul and told him that everyone on the ship would live. This was not merely a dream of an angelic messenger—the angel tangibly came to Paul.

Even more dramatically in Acts 12, Peter had a remarkable experience while asleep in prison, chained between two soldiers. An angel woke him and set him free from the chains and opened the prison doors. Peter supposed that he was having a dream or vision. He did not know it was "something more" until he was outside the prison and standing in the street.

VISITING HOME

There are also many examples in Scripture of people "caught up into heaven." Ezekiel, Daniel, Zechariah, Isaiah, Paul, John, and others experienced this phenomenon. In some instances, these men were uncertain whether their experience took place **"in the body or out of the body" (see II Corinthians 12:1–4).** They knew their experiences were real in that they did not merely take place in their minds. However, they were often so real that they could not tell whether it was their physical body or their spirit that had been taken into the heavenly realm.

Several years ago, I discovered a book long out of print called *Visions* by General William Booth, founder of the Salvation Army. I love to read about General Booth and the ministry's early exploits. History remembers Booth and his wife, Catherine, as fiery evangelists who mobilized the body of Christ to reach the harvest. However, a remarkable, less known element of Booth's life is that he was a modern mystic. He had many dreams and visions, and in some of them, he was caught up into heaven.

In *Visions*, Booth described heavenly experiences and face-to-face conversations with angels and saints from the past—even Jesus Himself. Many of these dreams were interactive, as though Booth was lucid during them. They were more real than a series of images and words flashing through his mind. He felt transported somewhere in these experiences.

Booth did not consider these experiences to be strange or unbiblical. Rather, he considered them an important part of his relationship with God. It is not surprising that the book has fallen out of print. Many would probably prefer to remember Booth the missionary rather than Booth the mystic.

WITH CHRIST IN HEAVENLY PLACES

In Ephesians 2:6, we are told that we are **"seated with Christ in heavenly places,"** implying that we have access to the heavenly realm. In Hebrews 4:16, we are given an invitation from God to **"come boldly to the throne of grace"** in heaven. Further, Hebrews 10:19–20 tells us to have **"boldness to enter the Holiest** [or the Holy of Holies] **by the blood of Jesus, by a new and living way which He consecrated for us, through the veil."** He has given us access and an invitation to experience heaven in a real way, including in our dreams.

Several years ago, I had an experience in the night that seemed to be "something more than a dream." I was standing on gently rolling hills in the early evening. A heavy, glowing fog covered the ground about knee-deep. I felt I was in a high place geographically. The dream was so vivid that I could smell the air and feel the fog's moisture.

A man approached and I immediately recognized him as a U.S. President from generations ago, although younger than the pictures I had seen of him. When he introduced himself, all I could say was, "But you're dead!" He replied, "Yes, but you're in heaven." With those words, I immediately became aware that I was indeed in heaven. This already vivid dream seemed to move from Technicolor to IMAX 3-D.

Soon a second man and a woman joined us. The President introduced them as his younger brother and his second wife. It seemed odd to me that this President from a conservative time in history would have been divorced and remarried—but then, the whole experience seemed "odd" to me.

The President began to tell me about his life. I asked him how he overcame a particular affliction when young because it was similar to an affliction in my life. He thoroughly answered my question and then stood over me, prophesying with great power. As he ministered to me, I became almost overwhelmed by the presence of God. He ended with the booming words, "You will fulfill your destiny!"

I awoke from the dream with vivid memories of every detail. I remembered exactly how he looked, the color of the scenery, and the feeling of the anointing as he ministered to me. Yet I could not remember the two most important things. First, I could not remember the answer to the question, "How did you overcome your affliction when you were young?" Second, I could not remember the many prophetic words he had spoken over me. I was troubled, but the Lord showed me that I would discover the answer to my questions by studying the life of this President. His life would be a prophetic word to me.

I began to research his life and discovered both missing elements of my dream. I read about how he overcame many challenges, including the one I had asked about. I discovered several vignettes from his life that "prophesied" to me and encouraged my pursuit of a high calling. Finally, I read about the brother whom I met in heaven, and I learned why the President had a second wife. His first wife contracted an illness and died prematurely. He remarried and started a family with his second wife.

I believe my experience in heaven was more than a dream. I was there "in the Spirit" and not "in the body," but it was somehow real, more tangible than a dream. I have had only a handful of this kind of encounter, but countless testimonies exist from others who report having the same experience.

God, grant us access to the "gate of heaven" You have opened to us.

15

THINKING SYMBOLICALLY

Dreams are often mysterious and require interpretation. This is because some dreams are communicated in visual or symbolic language. This book is not primarily about symbolism, but I felt it appropriate to include a chapter on "Thinking Symbolically." This is placed near the end of the book because the principles mentioned previously may be a better starting point for the journey of understanding dreams. Once we understand the supernatural nature of various categories of dreams, we are better positioned to interpret them.

DREAM HERMENEUTICS

The process of interpreting and understanding language is called "hermeneutics." We use hermeneutics every day. Any time we read something written by another or have a conversation with someone, we practice hermeneutics. We listen or read to "understand" the language being used—to know what is meant rather than merely what is said.

It has been said, in jest, that hermeneutics are especially important in husband-wife communication—we must be careful to understand what our spouse means when they speak, not only what they say. In like manner, to interpret dreams, we must ascertain the meanings of these nocturnal parables, not just the forthright communication. We are in need of sound "dream hermeneutics."

As Kevin Conner teaches in his book, *Interpreting the Scriptures*, the hermeneutic words in Scripture (words that pertain to interpretation or understanding of language) nearly all pertain to the interpretation of dreams and visions. Understanding and interpreting dreams is an important theme in biblical hermeneutics. The Bible is full of dreams and visions. It is also full of symbols: numbers, animals, and colors. These biblical symbols commonly show up in our dreams.

CATEGORIES OF SYMBOLS

In his book, *You May All Prophesy*, Steve Thompson lists three distinct categories of symbolism useful for our study and helpful in interpreting all prophetic revelation, including dreams. These basic categories are: Biblical Symbolism, Contemporary Symbolism, and Personal Symbolism. I will briefly comment on the relevance of each for understanding dreams.

BIBLICAL SYMBOLISM

Biblical symbols in our dreams may be the easiest to interpret. A simple concordance search can yield great insight as we read various appearances of a symbol in Scripture. For example, the number eight often speaks of new beginnings. This is because in the Bible, God preserved eight people in the ark when He made a new beginning for the earth. Also, God established a seven-day week, therefore the eighth day is the beginning of a new week.

Biblical symbols often build in significance as the narrative unfolds. In the first few chapters of Genesis, we find many symbols introduced: the Garden; the river; the tree; fruit; the serpent; the Seed (the Promised Redeemer); blood (animal sacrifice). Each of these symbols introduced in Genesis (The Book of Beginnings) is found throughout the Bible and culminates in the Book of Revelation. If you follow each of them through the Bible, you can see an unfolding revelation of their meaning. In hermeneutics, the principle that the understanding of a concept unfolds as it progresses in Scripture is called the Complete Mention Principle.

Let us consider the symbolism of "the Seed" in Genesis 3:15. This verse contains the first mention of God's plan of redemption. At the moment God "discovers" the sin of Adam and Eve, He promises a coming Seed who will crush the head of the serpent—even though His heel will be bruised in the process.

As we follow the symbol through the Bible, God promises that this Seed will come forth through Abraham and then through David. In the New Testament, we find that the Seed is Christ (see Galatians 3:16 and II Timothy 2:8) and He is bruised at the cross. The deceptively small serpent of the Garden has become the dragon in the Book of Revelation and he is crushed by the Seed (see Revelation 20:1–10).

PERSONAL SYMBOLISM

Just as we can identify symbols in Scripture to understand their meaning, we can also identify symbols in our own lives.

When I was a child, my aunt had a huge satellite dish in her backyard. I was fascinated as I imagined this dish receiving information all the way from the heavens. When I became a Christian and began to operate in the prophetic, I noticed that God often used the image of a satellite dish to speak to me about someone's prophetic gift. Prophetic gifting is a spiritual mechanism that allows one to receive messages from heaven, just like a satellite dish.

The tricky thing about personal symbols is that they do not always mean the same thing to everyone. For instance, if someone worked in military intelligence during the Cold War, the symbol of a satellite dish may speak to them of spiritual warfare. If someone works in radio, a satellite dish may have to do with broadcasting, rather than receiving information. To them, it may symbolize a platform to reach many people with a message.

This is one reason I put more emphasis on knowing the Lord than knowing symbolism when interpreting dreams. The Lord knows the meaning of every symbol He uses, and we should always ask Him for their interpretation. Further, we should ask questions of the dreamer, such as,

"What do you think of when you see a satellite dish?" Such questions may yield an effortless interpretation.

Over time, we each develop a vocabulary with the Lord. We begin to recognize the unique language He uses with us. Certain symbols take on a special meaning for us because God uses them time and time again. Similar to the Complete Mention Principle discussed above, we develop a history with God and understand His voice with increased clarity. We know what God is saying when we dream of a satellite dish because He has used this language with us in the past. God meets us where we are and He uses a language that we can understand.

CONTEMPORARY SYMBOLISM

Some dreams contain symbols that are neither biblical nor personal. Dreams may contain contemporary symbols. These are symbols that most people in a given culture would know at least a little bit about because they are common and contemporary.

If someone dreams of a fighter jet and they have no personal experience with them, they can still interpret the symbol. Most people understand that fighter jets are powerful vehicles that fly in the heavens to fight battles. Based on this general knowledge, we can begin to interpret. Depending on the context of the dream, the jet may symbolize a battle being fought in the heavens or maybe a person or ministry equipped for spiritual warfare. It could mean a lot of things, but we can interpret the symbol because everyone knows a little bit about fighter jets.

Examples of contemporary symbolism abound. If someone in a dream wears a badge, it may speak of authority because in our times, badges signify authority. If someone is dressed like a doctor, this may signify a healing gift, because in our culture their apparel is associated with healing.

Further, every culture has idioms and catchy sayings that have specific meaning to them. We should consider these when interpreting dream symbols. For example, to say that someone "bit off more than they can chew" means that they have taken on more than they can handle or that they are feeling overwhelmed. We also have a saying, "Let me chew on that for a while," which means, "allow me to process that." In light of these idioms, if someone dreams of losing all their teeth or having their mouth so full that their teeth begin to crumble, it may speak of feeling over-whelmed or having anxiety about a multitude of responsi-bilities. It could also mean that they are having difficulty processing events in their life.

If we are awakened to the potential meaning of sym-bols in the world around us, we will expand our ability to think prophetically and interpret dreams. We will expand our dream hermeneutics.

SEEING SYMBOLIC SCENARIOS IN YOUR WAKING LIFE

Symbolic scenarios play out in dreams, conveying a message to us. In the same way, symbolic scenarios some-times play out in our daily lives. God is involved in the minutia of our existence, and He often orchestrates events in order to speak to us. In this way, our lives become a living parable.

The lives of many biblical characters were prophetic and symbolic. They lived the scenes we read in Scripture and, for them, life became a parabolic. Consider the lives of Isaac and Joseph. Both men lived out a prophetic foreshadowing of the mission of Jesus. Isaac carried offering wood on his back as he walked the hill where his father was to sacrifice him. On that hill, a substitutionary sacrifice was provided. Joseph was rejected by his brothers, went through the crucible, was buried in the dungeon, and eventually was resurrected to sit on a throne of authority.

The prophets of old explained that events in their lives were signs from God. Isaiah prophesied that the birth of his children and even the names given to them were messages from God. Hosea understood that his life was a prophetic symbol to Israel. He endured the pain of marrying a prostitute, taking her back each time she was unfaithful. His life prophesied that God would redeem Israel, though His heart had been wounded by her harlotry.

These and many others in Scripture lived prophetic lives that communicated a message from God. Likewise, the experiences and coincidences in our lives are often speaking a message to us and to others. Think of the significance of marriage in Ephesians 5. A believer's marriage is meant to reveal the Great Mystery of Christ and the church. We would do well to remember this the next time we feel our marriage is under attack. The enemy intends more than to cause an argument. He seeks to corrupt the message our marriage is preaching.

Understanding these simple concepts helps us to think symbolically. If we will look for these living parables, we will find that God speaks constantly. A friend who trains people to identify the voice of God encourages students to pay attention to coincidences and unusual occurrences in their lives. He tells them to ask, "If this were a dream, what would it mean?" This question and the mindset it fosters will lead us down the path of prophetic understanding.

As we become more adept in identifying the symbolic language God uses in our waking lives, we will grow in dream interpretation, as well. As we become accustomed to the many ways God speaks, interpretation will become second nature.

SECTION

III

THE POWER OF DREAMS

Dreams have power to transform
lives and align people with destiny—
whether they know God or not.

16

DREAMS IN EVANGELISM

G od speaks, even to those who aren't listening. He reveals Himself to unbelievers in dreams. I have interpreted dreams in many settings: churches, New Age fairs, art festivals, flea markets, coffee shops, homes, etc. Time and time again, I have encountered people who do not know the Lord, yet they receive dreams from Him.

Biblical examples of this phenomenon abound. Remember Pilate's wife? God showed her that Jesus was a holy man on the eve of His crucifixion. Consider Pharaoh who dreamed of what would happen in Egypt fourteen years in advance. He did not understand his dream until a man of God gave him a revelatory interpretation. Prior to the dream, Pharaoh knew nothing of the God of Abraham. After Joseph interpreted the dream, Pharaoh gave glory to the true God, crediting the interpretation to Him and saying the Spirit of God was in Joseph. He then gave this Hebrew an exalted Egyptian name, Zaphenath-Paneah, which means "God speaks; He lives" (see Genesis 41:37–45).

We see the same pattern in the Book of Daniel. Nebuchadnezzar had a dream he did not understand, and God revealed the entire dream and its interpretation to Daniel. Nebuchadnezzar, a madman who threatened to kill every wise man in his kingdom, had a stunning change of heart. He prostrated himself before Daniel and said, **"Truly your God is the God of gods, the Lord of kings, and a revealer of secrets, since you could reveal this secret" (see Daniel 2:47).** He quickly promoted Daniel to ruler of all the Province of Babylon (see Daniel 2:46–49). This and a second dream paved the way for Nebuchadnezzar to turn to the Lord at the end of his life. The Psalm below sounds like it may have been written by King David, but it was the meditation of Nebuchadnezzar's heart at the time of his repentance:

> **I blessed the Most High and praised and honored Him who lives forever: for His dominion is an everlasting dominion, and His kingdom is from generation to generation.**
>
> **All the inhabitants of the earth are reputed as nothing; He does according to His will in the army of heaven and among the inhabitants of the earth. No one can restrain His hand or say to Him, "What have You done?"**
>
> **Now I, Nebuchadnezzar, praise and extol and honor the King of heaven, all of whose works are truth, and His ways justice. And those who walk in pride He is able to put down (see Daniel 4:34–35, 37).**

Like Pharaoh and Nebuchadnezzar, many who do not know God are receiving dreams from Him. For this reason, dreams are immeasurably valuable in evangelism. There is intense interest in dreams in all sectors of society. In fact, dream interpretation and similar terms rank high in Internet searches year after year. Dreamers are eager to listen to anyone offering insight into their dreams. As Christians, we have an unlimited source of insight.

INVITATIONS FROM HEAVEN

Several years ago I worked with a Filipino woman, whom I will call Perl. She had been raised Catholic but also held some superstitious beliefs. I talked with her about being "born again," explaining that Jesus said, "You must be born again to see the kingdom of heaven." She was not particularly interested, so I prayed that God would speak to her in dreams and place Filipino Christians in her life.

One morning Perl told of an experience she had as a child. She was at the market in Cebu and a witch approached her and took her hand. The witch proceeded to read her palm and tell Perl her life story, in advance. She said, "A man will come from a far-away land who will love you very much. You will be married and he will take you away from here. You will have three children but your firstborn will die. Your husband will live to be an old man, but you will die when you are of middle age."

Years after this experience, Perl met an American soldier stationed in Cebu. They fell in love, married, and traveled to the United States. They had three children, but the first died at birth. The entire prediction had come true thus far and Perl was fifty years old. She expected to die soon.

As I listened to the story, a holy anger rose up in me. I said, "Perl, I break that witch's curse off of you in the name of Jesus. I declare over you that you will live to see old age, and that the full purpose of God will be fulfilled in your life!" She said, "Uh, thank you" and went back to work.

The next morning, Perl came in and said, "Justin, I had a dream last night. I was walking around with many, many old women. I did not recognize any of them, but I knew that they were old." I immediately perceived the interpretation and replied, "Perl, this is God's confirmation to what I prayed over you yesterday. In this dream He is saying to you that you will see and walk in old age. That witch's curse is broken off of you." She was more than a little encouraged.

Soon after, Perl told me about a Bible study that she had begun attending with some friends. I asked her what kind of group it was and she said they were "born-agains,"only she said it like "bornagins"—one word rapidly pronounced. The group consisted of born-again Filipinos who had come out of the Catholic church. As the months ensued, Perl continued to attend the Bible study and even began to go to church with this group.

A month or so later she told me of another dream. She said, "I was being led down a hallway by a man whose face I could not see. At the end of the hall we found an open door. I had to step up onto a big rock to look through the door. When I looked through the door I found a beautiful world full of life and beauty. What in the world could that mean?"

I explained that this was a powerful dream. The face-less man was the Holy Spirit. He is the Faceless One, often hidden from our natural senses, and He is the One Who leads us. The hallway God led Perl down was the path towards the Rock and the Door—Jesus Christ. In the dream, when Perl stepped up on the Rock and peered through the Door, she saw a new life—a new world. This was an invitation to accept Christ and be born again.

I shared this interpretation with Perl. I am not sure she fully understood. However, she believed it was from God. Following these conversations about dreams, Perl viewed me as her pastor. She began coming to me for counsel and calling my wife and I for prayer when she needed support. God had answered my petitions for Perl and had powerfully impacted her life with dreams.

DREAMS OPEN DOORS

Interpreting a dream for someone who does not know Jesus can open the door to share the Gospel with them. Below are three unique ways in which dreams open doors to minister to unbelievers.

First, there are times when a dream is plainly from God and thus presents an occasion to share the Gospel. I have concluded an interpretation with, "It sounds like God is speaking to you in this dream. Have you ever considered trusting Jesus as your Savior and giving your whole life to Him?" This transitional question provides an opportunity for someone to receive salvation.

Second, at times a dream is clearly an attack from the devil. As we discussed in chapter eleven, dreams that are obviously full of fear, lust, or violence are usually demonically inspired. These too can be opportunities to lead someone to Jesus. I will typically say, "This dream seems dark. I believe the devil is influencing your dreams. Would you like to entrust your life to Jesus and come under His protection?" If the dreamer is willing to accept Christ, you can pray with them to break Satan's influence in their dreams.

Third, some dreams are from the soul and reveal the need for healing of the heart, as discussed in chapter nine. After interpreting these dreams I will say, "It sounds like your heart is in need of healing in this area. Jesus is the Healer and He would love to bring restoration to your soul. Would you like to commit your life to Him and ask Him to give you a renewed heart and a new beginning?"

Irrespective of a dream's source (God, the enemy, or the human soul), the interpretation can impact someone's eternity. Dreams are powerful in evangelism.

17

TREASURE YOUR DREAMS

Not every dream is from God. Some are no more than the unwinding and wandering of the mind as we sleep. I refer to these as "carnal dreams." If you fall asleep watching a monster truck rally on television, you may dream of barreling through the forest in the iconic blue *Bigfoot*, chasing the *Gravedigger*. You may not want to jump to an interpretive conclusion—that you are walking in a new anointing to pursue and stomp out the spirit of death. You should probably chalk the dream up to lingering excitement from seeing suped-up SUVs and trucks performing stunts and smashing cars.

That being said, unless a dream is obviously carnal we should ask God about it. Initially, some important dreams seem insignificant or incomprehensible. Only after inquiring of the Lord do we begin to understand them, and in some cases, remember vital scenes we have forgotten. Such dreams are like a chest full of gold hidden in a cardboard box. It would be reasonable to dismiss or ignore the box since it does not look like much on the outside. However, for those willing to go to the "trouble" of opening the box and looking inside, there is treasure to obtain.

As Proverbs 25:2 tells us, **"It is the glory of God to conceal a matter, but the glory of kings is to search out a matter."** God often conceals the glorious treasure He wants to give us, and it is our glory to be seekers of kingdom treasure. Only kings and queens and noble sons and daughters seeking Him will obtain the gold. It has been said that for something to be valuable it must be either rare or difficult to obtain. The treasures of the kingdom are not common or easy to obtain but these "true riches" are worth every ounce of energy spent searching for them.

THE GLORY OF KINGS

It is the glory of God to conceal a matter, but the glory of kings is to search out a matter. It is our glory to be seekers of kingdom treasure. We appear glorious to the earth when we embark on the lifelong quest of seeking God and His kingdom. We also experience the glory of God as we find what we are seeking. We are commanded to **"seek first the kingdom of God and His righteousness" (see Matthew 6:33).** When we do this, making His will and purposes the highest concern of our lives, God promises to take care of all of our earthly concerns (see Matthew 6:24–35). When we seek His righteousness, we are transformed into a different kind of humanity, a holy, supernatural, royal race. In this way we become the kings and queens we are created to be.

As we saw in preceding chapters, our dreams are precious gifts from God. If we believe this to be true, we must treasure our dreams—prize them as invaluable. We will now consider several practical ways that we can do this.

First, it is important to type or write out our dreams. Even our most vivid memories fade with time. Often I have been certain I would precisely remember a dream, only to discover that I could not recall important details. Further, as our dream lives activate and we dream more frequently, we will likely have dreams we do not understand. These may be some of the most significant, holding keys for understanding things to come. We may not understand them at the time because they are not yet relevant. God is alerting us to something coming, and He desires for us to pray into them or prepare in some way.

If we record our dreams, we can return to them when the time comes for their application. Recording our dreams also allows us to discover God's vocabulary that builds in them over time. Recurring themes and imagery take on personal meaning and our understanding of His intimate language to us becomes clearer.

In teaching about dreams through the years, I have been approached by those who cannot recall their dreams upon waking and thus cannot write them down. I often shared with them something I learned during my first year at MorningStar—**"The carnal mind is enmity against God; for it is not subject to the law of God, nor indeed can be" (Romans 8:7).** This means that the carnal part of our mind resists God. An unrenewed mind can block the remembrance of our dreams. In this case we must speak to our soul (the mind, will, and emotions) like David did in Psalm 42 and command the remembrance of our dreams.

We may also want to repent for allowing our soul to resist God's revelation to us.

A second way to treasure our dreams is seeking to interpret them. Bob Jones used to say that we must "unpack" a revelation. When God speaks to us, we treat His revelation as a gift box to unwrap, open, and fully examine the contents.

The more time we spend with a true revelation from God, the more we will gain from it. Think of the profound nature of the Scriptures. The written Word of God is inexhaustible in its potential for revelation. We can study the Bible our entire lives but only scratch the surface of all it contains. For eternity we will study the written Word of God, marveling at its beautiful revelation (see Isaiah 40:8, Matthew 24:35, and 1 Peter 1:25). In the same way, but to a lesser degree, the prophetic word God speaks in dreams is vast in its potential for revelation and application.

A third way we can treat our dreams as treasure is to act on them. God speaks with purpose. He does not give us dreams for our entertainment, but for our transformation and effectiveness as His servants: **"So shall My word be that goes forth from My mouth; it shall not return to Me void, but it shall accomplish what I please, and it shall prosper in the thing for which I sent it" (Isaiah 55:11).** God's word will be effective one way or another and He continually speaks to those faithful to act on it. If we are unfaithful with the word He speaks to us, He will speak the word to someone else who will value it enough to take action.

In certain seasons, I have had to repent for being unfaithful with my dreams. I had either stopped writing them down—evidence that I did not value them—or I had not sought to interpret or act on them. We must value the word of God and obey it.

Many years ago, I received a dream for an anointed leader who was also a friend. In the dream he was doing drugs and needed help to get free. I felt that the Lord wanted me to share the dream and offer my wholehearted support in his struggle. Insecure about sharing the dream with this leader because he was older and more influential than me, I procrastinated. When I finally did share the dream, I watered it down and sheepishly offered my help "if it is at all accurate." My friend took the dream out of context and said it referred to something completely unrelated. Within a year he was in rehab after being caught using hard-core drugs. He hurt his family and lost his church and many friends as a result. How might things have been different if I had faithfully shared the dream and offered my support with confidence and clarity?

If we desire to grow in authority and effectiveness in the kingdom of God, we must be faithful with what we are given. **"If you are faithful in little things, you will be faithful in large ones" (Luke 16:10, NLT).** God watches to see how we handle the small things. If we are faithful in small responsibilities, He can entrust us with greater ones. Let it be our prayer to hear God say to us what He said to the servant in Matthew 25:23: **"Well done, good and faithful servant. You have been faithful over a little; I will set you over much."**

PASSIONATE PURSUIT

The densest Bible passage on the gifts of the Spirit is I Corinthians 12–14. In these three chapters, we are told three times to desire and pursue spiritual gifts, especially the prophetic or revelatory ones (see I Corinthians 12:31, 14:1, and 14:39). God wants us to passionately pursue the Holy Spirit's activity in our lives, especially growth in our ability to hear His voice. We must keep pressing in for more prophetic revelation until we continually hear our Shepherd (see John 10:3–27). Jesus taught that if we persist in asking God to give us something, we will receive it. All we have to do is ask, seek, and knock (see Matthew 7:7–12 and Luke 11:9).

I began knocking, seeking, and asking for an active dream life after my first revelatory dream. Since that time, most significant events in my life have been foretold in dreams—every move to a new city, the births of my two children, the content of my "life message," my calling to write, and even my calling to pastor MorningStar Fellowship Church.

For years I dreamed of Rick Joyner teaching me to fly airplanes. At first, they were small two-seater planes and eventually, large 747 jumbo jets. I then dreamed I was the Maître d' at Rick's banquet hall, ensuring the food's quality and that the venue accurately represented him. Later I dreamed Rick made me the steward of his home, an enormous log cabin. I told no one but my wife of these dreams. I **"kept all these things and pondered them in [my] heart"** (see Luke 2:19) until the day I was asked to be pastor.

As I look back over my dream journals, I overflow with thanksgiving that God **"instructs me in the night seasons" (see Psalm 16:7).** He has told me of many things **"before they spring forth" (see Isaiah 42:9).** He has not left me as an orphan (see John 14:17–18) but has given me the Spirit of Truth.

Dreams are powerful for transforming our lives and aligning us with destiny—they are among the greatest gifts God has given to mankind. Dreams are one of the most common ways He spoke to His people in Scripture and throughout history. They are meant to be common in the lives of His people today.

Lord, speak to us in dreams and make us faithful stewards of all the treasures You give.

APPENDIX I –

DREAM EVALUATION AND INTERPRETATION WORKSHEET

On the following pages you will find a worksheet for evaluating and interpreting your dreams. The system of dream evaluation and interpretation presented here is based upon *Adventures in Dreaming: The Supernatural Nature of Dreams*. As this book teaches, not every dream merits interpretation. However, for those that do, this excerpt from the *Adventures in Dreaming: Dream Journal* will be a great help.

The questions asked on this worksheet are meant to provoke conversation with the Lord about your dreams and help you to categorize and understand them. Fill out each section as you pursue the interpretation and application of your dream. May your *Adventures in Dreaming* increase and abound!

DREAM EVALUATION AND INTERPRETATION WORKSHEET

Who was the dream for? _____

Summarize the dream: _____

_____

_____

_____

_____

Were there people in the dream who may have symbolized something and what may they have symbolized?_____

_____

_____

What symbols were in the dream and what do they mean? Could any symbol or statement in the dream be a "play on words?"_____

_____

_____

Was there anything in the dream that may have indicated the timing of fulfillment? Perhaps an event that will take place in the future? _____

_____

Were you sleeping in a new place or in proximity to a new person? _____

_____

How did you feel in the dream and upon waking? Was there an obvious mood or emotion experienced in the dre am?_____

_____

Have you been asking God for an answer to a question, or is there anything upcoming that He may be speaking to you about? _____

_____

Was this a recurring dream or theme? If so, what is being repeatedly emphasized? _____

_____

What is your interpretation of the dream? What is the message being communicated and/or what was accomplished in the spiritual realm through this dream? _____

_____

_____

_____

_____

_____

_____

How should you respond to the dream? Is there an action to take? Something you should seek the Lord about? Is the dream a call to repentance or perhaps a warning? Is it a call to enter into thanksgiving for a promise from God?

_____

_____

_____

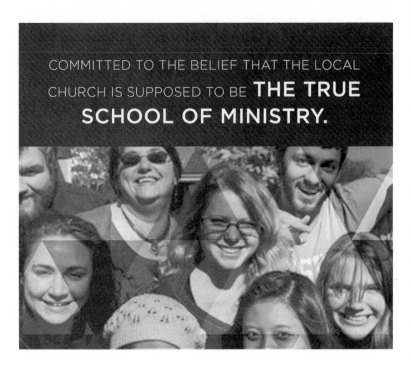

COMMITTED TO THE BELIEF THAT THE LOCAL CHURCH IS SUPPOSED TO BE **THE TRUE SCHOOL OF MINISTRY.**

In recent polls, less than 5% of people in an average congregation know what their gifts or callings are and only about 2% of those are actually equipped and functioning in their calling. **What body could possibly live if only 2% of its members were functioning? MSU exists to fulfill God's purpose for Christ-followers, the local church, and the body of Christ.**

For more information or to apply, visit:
MorningStarUniversity.com

 MorningStar Partners

The most powerful spiritual force since the first century is mobilizing. We are looking at the greatest potential impact for the gospel ever seen. We need Partners to help raise up and send the most high-impact ministries in church history.

Join with us to equip the body of Christ through our schools, missions, conferences, television shows, and publications. Your contributions are used to train and equip all ages in their prophetic gifting. You can become a MorningStar Partner with a regular contribution of any amount, whether it is once a month or once a year.

Partnership Benefits:
- Receive monthly newsletters with rich, timely content from Rick Joyner and others
- Participate in live video webinars featuring key prophetic voices
- Connect with Partners and staff at exclusive Partner events and in our Koinonia Lounge
- Enjoy a complimentary subscription to the MorningStar Journal
- Save money with special discounts on products, hotel rooms, conferences, and more

Become a MorningStar Partner Today:

MStarPartners.org

or call
1-803-547-8495